PRAISE FOR *DO WHAT YOU SAY YOU'LL DO*

This is an important book for anyone trying to understand what the hell leadership means today. In a world full of competing pet theories and ongoing questioning of the meaning and value of leadership, Tansley shines a light on what it means to be a successful leader in this day and age.

While Do What You Say You'll Do *is as well grounded in research and theory as any serious management text, its common sense approach and easy to read style make it accessible to both experts and practitioners alike.*

Tansley's advice that normal people can be leaders is gold. Leadership is not some unique gift of the gods given to a blessed few. Tansley's insights demonstrate that almost anyone can lead if they keep it real and learn a bit about themselves and others. Whether you want to lead well or be well led, this book will help you understand how to bring out the best in yourself and others in a way that is authentic, permanent and real.

—Dr Brendan Shaw, Assistant Director General, International Federation of Pharmaceutical Manufacturers and Associations, Geneva, Switzerland.

A thought provoking and insightful read. Tammy has distilled the best in contemporary leadership thinking in a very concise and approachable way. Highly recommended for both aspiring and experienced leaders.

—*Martin Wandmaker, Head of Human Resources, Automotive Holdings Group*

Do What You Say You'll Do *sets the new leader up to create positive impact across all their zones of influence. The author shares a great toolkit that will enable leaders to adopt the mindsets, drivers, attributes, behaviours and skills required to lead self and others to great success. An incredible resource for all new leaders.*

—*Paula Flynn Global Executive Coach and Leadership Development Consultant*

DO WHAT YOU SAY YOU'LL DO

And other tools to LEAD courageously

Copyright © 2015 by Tammy Tansley

All rights reserved.

Published in Australia by Tammy Tansley Consulting Press.

The moral rights of the author have been asserted.

www.dowhatyousay.com.au

National Library of Australia Cataloguing-in-Publication entry

Creator: Tansley, Tammy, author.

Title: Do what you say you'll do : and other tools to lead courageously / Tammy Tansley.

ISBN: 9780994305916 (paperback)

Subjects: Leadership. Executive ability. Self-actualization (Psychology) Achievement motivation. Success. Leadership--Interviews.

Dewey Number: 658.4092

All rights reserved. Except as permitted under the *Australian Copyright Act 1968* (for example a fair dealing for the purposes of study, research, criticism or review) no part of this book may be reproduced, stored in a retrieval system, communicated or transmitted in any form or by any means without prior written permission. All inquiries should be made to the publisher above.

Printed in the United States of America

Jacket Design: Reese Spykerman

Book Design: Kelly Exeter

First Edition

For Alex and my girls — with love and gratitude

GUEST CONTRIBUTORS

Many thanks to the following who have contributed their words and wisdom.

David Koutsoukis is a leadership and team development specialist who helps leaders build exceptional teams through speaking, training and consulting. He has been a professional speaker for more than ten years, has twice been named WA Speaker of the Year and is a past president of the National Speakers Association of Australia.

Amanda Alldrick is an ICF Credentialed coach who practices Ontological Coaching. She has a passion for partnering with clients to bring out their best, to recognise underlying beliefs, core truths and stories that run in their lives and influence behaviours and choices. Amanda's strength lies in relationship building and partnering with others to drive change in behaviours. At the heart of this is a coaching practice that underpins the foundation for the change process.

Justin Miles is the Managing Director of The Talent Workshop, an organisation focused on developing people and teams to reach their full performance potential. Justin has more than 25 years executive experience in industries ranging from consumer goods, through to retail, manufacturing, government and lifestyle apparel industries.

INTERVIEWS

Many thanks to the following who agreed to be interviewed and included in this book:

Brian Cook is a 5 time AFL Premiership CEO, who talks about leadership in high performance organisations. A lifetime spent in this high-pressure industry has resulted in so many interesting experiences and shaped some interesting life opinions!

Sonja Cox graduated with a high distinction in Criminal Justice Administration, and then commenced work in Corrective Services Victoria before relocating to WA. Sonja has had a distinguished career in the WA Public Sector for the past 20 years in various leadership positions. In 2013 Sonja won the WA Telstra Business Woman of the Year and was acknowledged for her work in a complex environment and commitment to self, her young family and the community.

Maggie Dent is an author, educator, and parenting and resilience specialist who has written seven books full of common-sense wisdom on parenting and life. Her diverse career history includes teaching, youth and family counselling, palliative care and funeral services, and radio announcing. She is the proud mother of four sons and one precious granddaughter.

Dr Penny Flett was born in England, schooled in several countries, and studied medicine in Adelaide. Penny has spent her working life engaged with people....first as a doctor, and then working to change services for our society's elders, and younger people with challenging conditions. Leadership for the better has long been her focus, including frequently challenging the status quo!

The Australian Financial Review and Westpac named **Holly Ransom** in 2012's '100 Most Influential Australian Women' list. She was awarded the Young Western Australian of the Year and Young Volunteer of the Year in 2012. She became the world's youngest Rotary President in 2012. She is a sought after keynote speaker and has represented Australia in global summits.

Donny Walford is an experienced Non Executive Director and CEO of public unlisted companies and various strategic boards in the Finance, Defence and Government industry sectors with specific expertise in Strategy, Finance, Strategic Marketing and building businesses. The founder and Managing Director of DW Behind Closed Doors Pty Ltd (BCD) and DW Bottom Line Pty Ltd (Bottomline) Transition Strategists™, Donny has an extensive background at Executive and senior management levels in banking, finance, business services, government and human resources.

Professor Fiona Wood is one of Australia's most innovative and respected surgeons and researchers. A highly skilled plastic and reconstructive surgeon and world leading burns specialist, she has pioneered research and technology development in burns medicine. She was awarded Member of the Order of Australia in 2003, the Australian Medical Association's 'Contribution to Medicine' award in 2003, the 2003 and 2004 West Australian of the Year and 2005 Australian of the Year. She was voted Australia's Most Trusted Person for six successive years (2005-2010) and has been recognised as an Australian Living Treasure.

CONTENTS

DO WHAT YOU SAY YOU'LL DO

And other tools to LEAD courageously

*A guide for first time leaders and those
reinventing their leadership style*

TAMMY TANSLEY

TAMMY TANSLEY CONSULTING
AUSTRALIA

INTRODUCTION

In writing this book, I interviewed a number of leaders to seek their wisdom and experience on what leadership means. When I interviewed Brian Cook, the five time AFL premiership CEO, I asked him if there was one thing that emerging leaders could do that would make a difference to the way they lead.

His answer was as simple as it was powerful:

Do What You Say You'll Do.[1]

Indeed!

This piece of wisdom not only provided the title of this book, it also nicely illustrates the approach the book takes—practical wisdom that you can implement now!

So you have a new leadership role. Congratulations! You probably feel pretty excited about this. You've put in the hours and done your hard yards over a number of years.

But it might also feel daunting. You're worried: does leadership mean that suddenly you have to develop extraordinary charisma and start delivering Martin Luther King–type speeches? And how do you begin building your team? Particularly given that just a few days ago, these guys were your colleagues.

A quick search on amazon.com shows that over 172,000 books are dedicated to leadership alone. So why another book on this topic? In my 20-plus years of working with and coaching leadership teams and individual leaders, my clients have often commented on how it would be so useful if a book existed that could take them on their leadership journey: a bit like their own personal coach. *Do What You Say You'll Do* lists the fears, concerns and questions that many of my clients share with me.

Thought leader and prolific author Seth Godin says in his book *Linchpin*: that "telling people leadership is important is one thing. Showing them step by step precisely how to be a leader is impossible."[2]

Whilst that is certainly true, wouldn't it be good if there was a book that showed you different ways of doing things as a leader, that gave you some simple tips and tools, and shared wisdom from those who've gone before? Well, this is that book! *Do What You Say You'll Do* will give you the tools that great leaders use, and show how you can use them too.

There are a lot of misconceptions around what leadership actually is. Many people have the Richard Branson style of leadership in mind—and think that it's unattainable. This book will debunk the myths that there is only one sort of leadership personality, with charisma and good looks, and that leadership is about being in a fancy office with a fancy suit.

This book will also address these common fears:

- I'm not good enough: when will they discover I'm a fraud?

- How do I give feedback to my mates?
- I *hate* speaking in front of a group …
- How do I manage expectations, both good and bad?
- What if I fail?
- Do I need to be tough?

Do What You Say You'll Do will give you practical tools that will help you plan how to lead your team. A lot of new leaders just don't know where to start and then it all becomes too hard.

This book will tell you all about the things that great leaders do—and that you can do too. It will give you the skills to examine yourself and your situation, and let you know how you can lead in a pragmatic and conscious manner. It will allow you to address any fears you have about your new role.

This book will enable you to find your authentic voice: What makes you who you are? It will also play to your strengths: What will give you the courage to lead? This book is not about making you into something that you're not. It's about giving you tools that great leaders use and showing you that no matter who you are, you can use them too.

In each section, simple and quick Take a Moment exercises will allow you to make this about you and your journey. If you're like me, you'll be inclined to read on past these, thinking you'll come back to them at the end. But because this book *is* about you and *your* journey and your thinking, it's much better if you do the exercises then and there, even if you don't write your responses down. Take a moment to think about them before reading on.

Each section also has a number of Sticky Messages: the key points to reflect on.

Part One is all about the what and the why: What is a leader and why does any of this matter? Part Two is a series of tools that you can use (starting now). Part Three takes a look at your mindset. Part Four is all about looking out for you.

So, here's the thing. You now have a choice. You can be a manager of people or a leader of people. Whether you're leading your first team in an organisation, or you've been promoted to coach a sports team, or you're setting up a not-for-profit movement to galvanise community action, the principles are the same. And the good news is that you can do it.

Having said all that, there will be times that are difficult, because true leadership isn't always easy. From time to time you'll feel uncomfortable, vulnerable and outside of your comfort zone.

True leadership involves something special. You can create something extraordinary. However leadership is defined for you and your circumstances, you can make a conscious choice about how you approach the path ahead. *Do What You Say You'll Do* will excite and inspire you with examples of all kinds of successful leaders who have travelled the path that you're on. This book contains many wise anecdotes, stories, quotes and interview responses from some leaders both here in Australia and overseas.

It will also point you to some great resources to whet your appetite and further your knowledge. Please visit www.dowhatyousay. com.au to enhance your learning journey. Remember that a book such as this can only skim the surface of these topics, so reading more on the areas that interest you will help round out your knowledge in a particular area.

Finally, the one thing that leaders lack most of all is time. So, *Do What You Say You'll Do* gives you what you need to know in bite-sized chunks. It's designed so that you can read it one section at a time, whether on public transport on the way to work, or at your desk while you're eating lunch, or lying in bed at night reading your Kindle or tablet.

So, let's get started.

PART 1
Debunking the Leadership Myth

So, What is a Leader?

*While leadership is hard to define, its absence is
keenly felt.*

—Matt Church

Before we delve into your journey, there are a few absolute
fundamentals that we need to get sorted. Firstly, we need to
understand who and what a leader is.

It's true that some pretty extraordinary people have achieved
things beyond most of our wildest dreams and expectations.
Think of Gandhi, who led India to independence, and inspired
civil rights and freedom movements across the world. Think of
Martin Luther King, Jr. Think of Nelson Mandela. Think of the
Dalai Lama. Or Burmese Freedom fighter Daw Aung San Suu
Kyi and African–American Civil Rights activist Rosa Parks.

Then think of Richard Branson, who created the Virgin business
empire, or Steve Jobs, who was so instrumental in building the
Apple brand. Think of Bill Gates. Or Sheryl Sandberg: author
of *Lean In.*

When you think of the words "leader" and "leadership", these are the
people who often spring to mind. And so they should. These people
have done extraordinary things, created empires and left legacies.

Their achievements are also unattainable for most of us.

When leadership is defined as something global—something that changes millions of lives, something that radically alters the direction of history—this sets up daunting expectations that most of us will never be able to achieve.

However, every single one of us is given opportunities to make a difference in our own lives: to be leaders in our own communities, businesses, sporting groups and not-for-profits. Each of us has the ability to lead courageously.

To model leadership on the inspirational is great if it truly provides inspiration, but not if it makes it seem all too hard, all too out of reach, too daunting.

The wonderful Maggie Dent, parenting and early childhood expert, author and speaker has this to say on leadership:

> *Leadership can be seen as performing one or more acts of leading that affects human behaviour so as to influence a group of people toward a vision or goal.*

She goes one step further by saying:

> *Exceptional leadership does this with one other key attribute—it aims to achieve a goal for the greater good of all and for the positive growth of individuals.*[3]

This book is about how true leadership is completely within your grasp. How you don't need to own an island or have millions following you to call yourself a leader. There's no prerequisite that you need to comply with or leadership stereotype that you have to fit into. You don't need to look a certain way, dress a certain way or hold a PhD to be a leader.

You have everything you need within you, including the courage to start right now. This book will give you the tools that great leaders use and show you how you can use them too. But you do need to use them. You do need to show up.

Seth Godin sums it up well:

> *You can't look at the end result —at the Richard Bransons or Maria Popovas —and say, 'Well they have that thing and I don't.' They got that thing by showing up.[4]*

TAKE A MOMENT

Take a moment now to reflect on whom you consider to be a leader: in private enterprise, in politics, in the community sector, in medical research. Write their names here, using a sticky note or lead pencil if you don't like writing in books.

So, What Is a Leader? And What Does It Mean to Lead?

The names above are powerful examples of *who* is defined as a leader, but they don't define *what* a leader is and what it means to lead either a team or an issue.

From the Definition from the Collins Paperback English Dictionary (1990)

Leader (n)

a person who rules, guides or inspires others.

Or this one from the *Concise Oxford English Dictionary* (1984)

To Lead (v)

guidance given by going in front

The great thing about all of these definitions is that there's nothing in any dictionary about having to own an island or earn a PhD or own a billion-dollar company. There are no prerequisites for who can be a leader. There are no barriers to entry.

This book will take you on a journey that shows you how you can use your talents, your strengths, your personality and your circumstances to lead, and to create your own leadership style that meets the definitions of "leader" and "to lead".

You can lead from anywhere, from any position, from any point in any organisation. You can provide leadership to a team *or* on an issue. And you can apply this to any aspect of your life (be it coaching a sports team or taking on a leadership role in a voluntary organisation).

In his 2014 TED talk, best selling author and leadership thinker, Simon Sinek says:

> *Leadership is a choice. It is not a rank. I know many people at the senior-most levels of organisations who are absolutely not leaders. They are authorities and we do what they say because they have authority over us, but we would not follow them. And I know many people who [are] at the bottoms of organisations who have no authority and they are absolutely leaders, and this is because they have chosen to look after the person to the left of them, and they have chosen to look after the person to the right of them. This is what a leader is.*[5]

STICKY MESSAGES :: A VERY SHORT RECAP

- There is no formula for leadership.

- Leadership doesn't come from position or authority or rank. It comes from influence.

- *You* can lead irrespective of your place in the organisation. As Simon Sinek says, leadership is a choice.

RESOURCES

You can listen or watch Simon Sinek's 2014 TED Talk on *Why Good Leaders Make You Feel Safe* and view other resources on www.dowhatyousay.com.au

The Impact of Leadership

You are here to make a difference, to either improve the world or worsen it. And whether or not you consciously choose to, you will accomplish one or the other.

—*Richelle E. Goodrich*

So Why Does Any of This Matter?

As with most things in life, good leadership matters both for the impact it can have when it's done well and for the disproportionately bad impact it can have when done badly. Matt Church, author of *Amplifiers,* sums it up well:

> *If you have ever worked for a jerk, you know the detrimental impact a bad leader can have on a group. Nothing saps the energy of good people more quickly than bad leaders. These are the adults who have never grown up. These people somehow work their way through the rank and file, and end up in positions of influence. They bully, they blame, and they basically allow their personal pathology to drive their leadership behaviours.[6]*

Some real-life examples of questionable leadership behaviours:

- The ex-military boss who would call out to his team members at the top of his voice, "You've failed";

- The boss who bullied his team with ridiculous micromanagement and over-the-top requests;

- The boss who, after a full-day session on leadership with her entire team present, stormed out without a word of thanks to the presenters or any final wrap-up comments to the team;

- The boss who was having an extramarital affair and asked his subordinate to lie for him when he didn't come home one night after being with his lover;

- The boss who told his team member that the only thing going for her was her eyebrows;

- The boss who could never be pinned down to any decision and would deny making a decision at a later point;

- The boss who asked his team member what she was wearing under her skirt;

- The boss who left photos of his overseas mistress in the flipbook that he went through with his staff member;

- The boss who had boozy Friday afternoon lunches, and for thirteen consecutive weeks fired someone on his return to the office.

Many of these examples are years old, demonstrating the lasting impact and power that poor leadership can have. Sadly, the list goes on and on, with example after example of questionable judgment and poor behaviour. Just as I was finishing off this book, along came the example of the CEO who offered his employee a breast enhancement. You honestly could not make this stuff up![63]

In fact, when Stanford professor Bob Sutton recently wrote of the original *Harvard Business Review* article that led to his 2007 book *The No Asshole Rule*, he said that despite writing longer and more well-researched articles since, he has yet to receive such a strong response—and that to this day, the emails continue. He has now received over a thousand examples of poor leadership behaviour.[7]

The Contagion Effect

We've probably all worked for or heard about "leaders" who act like this. The effects can be devastating for those below. Another worrying thing is that these "leaders" don't just affect the people who directly report to them: they have an effect on the whole organisation.

Here's Tony Schwartz, a *Harvard Business Review* blogger, author of *Be Excellent at Anything* and CEO of The Energy Project, who says that "leaders, by virtue of their authority, exert a disproportionate impact on the mood of those that they supervise ... Negative emotions spread fast, and they're highly toxic."[8]

The problem with bad or absent leadership is not just that it hurts others, but also the multiplying effect of the impact it has on the organisation. Others can view the behaviour of one bad leader as an excuse for their own mediocre leadership behaviours.

The Cost of Poor Leadership Behaviours

Leadership authors and experts Lombardo and Eichinger put it succinctly ".. the penalty for less-than-able leadership is huge, as is the payoff when leadership is present."[9]

Poor leadership isn't just bad for morale; it also affects productivity, customer service, employee turnover, innovation and engagement. Every single one of these elements has a direct link to the bottom line in organisations and more broadly across the nation.

The 2012 McKell Institute Report, *Understanding Productivity, Australia's Choice*, had this to say: "Superior management performance is positively linked to expanded sales, market valuation, employment growth and productivity…It is increasingly recognised that the development of leadership and management skills is crucial to the improvement of Australia's productivity performance."[10]

In their 2010 book, *Manager Redefined*, Tom Davenport and Stephen Harding analysed 40 global companies over a three-year period and found that those who had a highly engaged employee population had a significantly better financial performance than those with less engaged employees. They then analysed the drivers of engagement and found that the number one engagement driver was the perceived strength and performance of senior leaders. They went on to say that the behaviour and effectiveness of direct supervisors is also woven through the list of factors that affect employee engagement.[11]

The global research firm Gallup, which has now conducted eight meta-analysis research studies, backs up this research. Their *State of the Global Workplace Report 2013* confirmed once again that there was a strong and well established link between employee engagement and a series of key performance outcomes including: customer ratings, profitability, productivity, turnover (for high- and low-turnover organizations), safety incidents, shrinkage (theft), absenteeism, patient safety incidents and quality (defects).

The report goes on to state that:

> *Gallup's research also shows that companies with engaged workforces have higher earnings per share (EPS) and seem to have recovered from the recession at a faster rate" and that "organizations with a critical mass of engaged employees outperformed their competition, compared with those that did not maximize their employees' potential.*[12]

And then there are the legal and brand implications.[13] The increasing emphasis on anti-bullying has been costing companies big in terms of both payouts and damage to their brands: anyone remember the David Jones debacle of 2010 where the CEO resigned suddenly in the wake of allegations around his behaviour?

The Story of the Grocery Store CEO

While I was writing this book, a huge furore hit the media. It started off as something quite small. A grocery chain in New England, USA had its CEO, Arthur T. Demoulas, ousted. What happened next was quite extraordinary.

The workers refused to deliver fresh produce to the 71 stores, meaning the shelves were left empty. Of course, then customers began leaving—partly because they couldn't buy fresh food, but, interestingly, also as a sign of protest.

So, the employees were prepared to stand up for Demoulas, losing wages in the process. It's quite astonishing, as CEOs are often accused of sitting in their ivory towers and not being approachable.

The story makes more sense when you hear the employees describe Demoulas, as they have done here:

> *Employees said it was their allegiance to Demoulas that kept them united. Demoulas is beloved by the workers not only for offering generous benefits—including a profit-sharing plan—but also for stopping to talk to workers, remembering birthdays and attending funerals of employees' relatives.*

> *"He'll walk into a warehouse and will stop and talk to everyone because he's genuinely concerned about them," said Joe Schmidt, a store operations supervisor. "He cares about families, he asks about your career goals, he will walk up to part-timers and ask them about themselves. To him, that cashier and that bagger are just as important as the supervisors and the store management team."*

> *Schmidt said Demoulas once called a store manager after he heard the man's daughter was critically injured in a car crash. Demoulas wanted to know whether the hospital she was in was giving her the best*

> care possible. "Do we need to move her?" he asked. "He is just a good man," Schmidt said.[14]

The revolt not only led to Demoulas being reinstated, but also led to millions of dollars lost from the company in the intervening six weeks.

This is yet another example of leadership having a direct impact on the bottom-line.

Personal Career Derailers

All of that is fine and dandy—but that is all at an organisational level. Let's get personal. What's in it for *you* to lead well?

Dr Lois Frankel, best-selling author of: *Nice Girls Don't Get Rich* and leadership coach, sums this up well with the following story:

> *Sara was an engineer with an outstanding record .., when she was promoted to manager of her department. Although she was able to produce high-quality results for six years she was an individual contributor, she's currently floundering in her role as leader.[16]*

Sara's story is a familiar one. I have seen it played out in every organisation that I have ever worked with, and no doubt you have seen it too. The accountant who is hard working and clever and analytical and who quickly climbs the ladder, only to come unstuck when he is put in charge of his first team. The laboratory technician who is tagged 'high potential' and made a team leader, only to find that she has fantastic technical skills but very limited leadership skills. And whilst the analytical fields (engineering, finance, quality) get tarred with these stories, the reality is true for every area of organisational life.

Leadership requires specific skills. You can't just keep doing what you always did. Learning the tools that this book provides will give you an excellent head start.

A recent Harvard Business Review study analysed the competencies required at every level of leader. There were two interesting points from the study:

1. That the top four competencies matter whatever level job you're in (new leader to very senior, experienced executive)

2. That there are some competencies which whilst not needed now will be critical in the next level, and being able to demonstrate those competencies in advance provides evidence that you may be successful at the next level.[17]

One of the key things I talk about in this book is development (both yours and your team's), so I like the concept that we are always working on the skills we need now, but with one eye to the future.

For more information on leadership competencies and derailers, an excellent resource is *For Your Improvement*, a book that provides practical exercises on how to improve specific competencies and address particular career derailers.[18]

Whichever way you view it, bad leadership costs. It can cost emotionally and financially. It can show in the lack of engagement and high turnover. It can show in poor quality customer service. It can show in the profit and earnings of an organisation. And it can impact on an organisation's reputation and brand.

The good news, though? This isn't a book about bad or absent leadership. It's a book about how you can summon your courage to act in a way that amplifies all those very same things for good rather than evil!

TAKE A MOMENT

Think about the leaders you've come across to date—not just at work, but also in sporting and community clubs. Was there one who seemed particularly good or bad? What made them so good or so bad? How long ago was this? Why has the memory stood the test of time? Most importantly, what was the impact of that person's leadership on you and the organisation?

STICKY MESSAGES :: A VERY SHORT RECAP

- Poor leadership comes in many guises.

- Poor leadership and its attendant behaviours are toxic and contagious within organisations.

- Poor leadership costs in terms of personal impact, organisational productivity and the bottom line.

- The connection between leadership and the bottom line is very well established.

- One of the main career derailers has been identified as the inability to lead.

RESOURCES

There are plenty of great resources on www.dowhatyousay.com.au including links to Dr Frankel's article and the HBR article on the competencies required for leadership.

How Leading is Different from Managing

*Management gets a bad name in many business
books. It's represented as a kind of cardigan-wearing,
boring compliance function ... We need managers
to get things done ... Managers are brilliant at
activating the people around them to get the job
done; they marshal resources and get people focused.*

—Matt Church

An important distinction needs to be made between leading
and managing. Over the years there have been mountains of
articles, books and research dedicated to drawing this line. Here
the renowned best-selling author and leadership expert John
P. Kotter has nailed the difference between management and
leadership:

> *... Management is a set of well-known processes,
> like planning, budgeting, structuring jobs, staffing
> jobs, measuring performance and problem-solving,
> which help an organization to predictably do what
> it knows how to do well. Management helps you to
> produce products and services as you have promised,
> of consistent quality, on budget, day after day,*

week after week. In organizations of any size and complexity, this is an enormously difficult task. We constantly underestimate how complex this task really is, especially if we are not in senior management jobs. So, management is crucial—but it's not leadership.

Leadership is entirely different. It is associated with taking an organization into the future, finding opportunities that are coming at it faster and faster and successfully exploiting those opportunities. Leadership is about vision, about people buying in, about empowerment and, most of all, about producing useful change. Leadership is not about attributes, it's about behavior. And in an ever-faster-moving world, leadership is increasingly needed from more and more people, no matter where they are in a hierarchy. The notion that a few extraordinary people at the top can provide all the leadership needed today is ridiculous, and it's a recipe for failure.

It's important to note that we need both. As Kotter says:

Some people still argue that we must replace management with leadership. That is obviously not so; they serve different, yet essential purposes. We need superb management. And we need more superb leadership...

Until we realise that we're not talking about management when we speak of leadership, all we will try to do when we need more leadership is work harder to manage. At a certain point, we end up with over-managed and under-led organisations which are increasingly vulnerable in a fast-moving world.[19]

During my 20-plus years of working in organisations, I've come across managers who are quite spectacular. They can muster the resources, produce the product and ensure the quality is spot on. But they don't necessarily empower or inspire. They don't look to the future; they're more concerned with what's happening today. But let's be really clear: we *need* these people. They are critical for organisations to get stuff done.

When I write this chapter, I am thinking of one particular Manager who I came to know very well over a long period of time. He was hardworking, passionate about the business, a technical and operational expert in his field. He was sought out for his views on product and quality issues. He was also a thoroughly nice man.

Over the years, the organisation had tried hard to mould him more into a leader; he was sent off on leadership programmes and development programmes. But in all honesty, his heart was never in it. He only ever wanted to be responsible for making sure that the product got made, on time, on spec and at the right quantity every day. He was happy problem solving when things went wrong. He was happy organising rosters and sorting out who did what to make the whole operation run like clockwork. He was happy making sure that the reporting got done. He liked his team and was popular and kind. He just didn't want to be setting direction or inspiring his team towards a common purpose or any other aspect of leadership. He was a Manager, and a very good one at that.[20]

But this book isn't about management. It's about leadership.

To manage you need to have positional power of some sort; you need to be a "manager" of something or someone. If you're reading this book, then you might be a manager wanting to do more than just manage, or you might be someone who isn't a manager but wants to lead by influence. Or you might be taking a leadership role by taking a leadership position on a cause rather than leading people.

The last point is an important one. We often think that leading is just another word for managing a team. But leadership *can* be about taking a position on something and influencing within the wider community. If we think back to the leaders named in the first section, only those in the corporate world could be said to be "managing staff"—the others, well, they've been leaders because they've exerted influence on the world.

As an example, Maggie Dent is an author and speaker who isn't in charge of a large organisation. What she does do, though, is provide leadership on an issue that she is passionate about. As she says:

> *I had an inspired moment where I thought, "I need to step up and gather these different voices from parents, early childhood educators and allied health professionals and take these messages to the bureaucratic powers that be so that we can have conversations to stop what is unhelpful and unhealthy for children."*[5]

That's leadership in action.

Another illustration of this is the role of the shop steward or union representative. I have come across a number of examples during my career in industrial relations where individuals have taken a strong leadership stance on a particular issue that they believed strongly in. Arguably, the union representative has no formal organisational power, but in my experience, those that approached an issue with a positive leadership stance led to a better outcome than the more typical adversarial and rabble-rousing approach.

TAKE A MOMENT

What's your current situation? Are you managing a team but want to do more? Maybe you have been identified as a leader of tomorrow. Maybe you don't have anyone currently reporting to you, but want to take a leadership role within your organisation.

Or perhaps you want to take a leadership position on an issue. What is that issue and why do you need to take a leadership stance on it?

Think about your current position. Are you ready to make a conscious decision to do something different? Something more? Are you ready to find your courage?

STICKY MESSAGES :: A VERY SHORT RECAP

- Management and leadership are different. The delineation is important to understand.

- Being a manager within an organisation is a key role, and should not be downplayed.

- You can be a leader within an organisation without actually managing anyone.

- Leadership doesn't need to be about leading a team of people in an organisation. You can be a leader through your "thought leadership" or your leadership on a cause or issue.

RESOURCES

There are plenty of great resources on www.dowhatyousay.com.au including some excellent articles on the difference between management and leadership.

Characteristics of a Leader

Many times people are placed in leadership roles and inherently believe that their teams will follow them due to the title on their business card and not the substance of their character. Leadership is as much about being the person that people want to follow as it is about knowing where the team is headed.

—Gary Peterson

There are as many books devoted to the characteristics of a good leader as there are on the differences between a leader and a manager! Some of the characteristics that are mentioned over and over again are:

- Flexibility
- Empathy
- Great communication skills
- Courage, tenacity and patience
- Humility and presence
- Taking responsibility and accountability
- Delegation skills

- Building trust
- Building their team up rather than pulling them down
- Honesty and integrity
- Stability
- Consistency
- Generosity
- Inspiring and motivating
- Results driven
- Problem solver

Many of these characteristics will be addressed in the following sections, along with ways that you can develop them by building on your innate strengths. And if you're looking for more resources, *For Your Improvement* is a wonderful tool that gives you practical ways to build your competencies.[18]

On the flipside, you may see characteristics such as:

- Micromanages
- Has an inconsistent direction or vision, or an approach that causes confusion
- Pits one person against another (or one team against another) in the name of "performance"
- Rarely gives constructive feedback
- Is a bad communicator
- Has a big ego

- Takes the credit but not the blame

- Is quick to find fault and slow to praise

- Gossips about team members

- Plays favourites among the team

- Has very little empathy or thought for others

- Keeps things close to their chest

- Keeps people small rather than encouraging them to stand up and be the best they can be

- Over-promises and under-delivers

- Is closed and rarely opens up or shows vulnerability

- Takes things very personally— you are either with them or against them

What's Missing from the List?

Interestingly, there are two leadership characteristics that are widely thought to be essential but that don't appear in the list above.

Firstly, *charisma (n)*, which is defined as:

> compelling attractiveness or charm that can inspire devotion in others. "He has tremendous charisma and stage presence". "Some managers acquire authority through their personal charisma"
>
> a divinely conferred power or talent.[21]

Many leaders who have charisma in bucket loads aren't such great leaders, while plenty don't possess as much charisma but are still extraordinary. When it comes to the latter group, I'm thinking of great leaders like the Dalai Lama. Arguably, there are people who are much better at speaking, at rousing a crowd—and yet few would argue about the Dalai Lama's mesmerising leadership prowess.

The second characteristic is a deep knowledge of the area in which the person is a leader. Although it may seem counterintuitive, this characteristic is not a requirement for leadership. In fact, some would argue that while experience brings a degree of credibility, the ability to ask the "stupid" questions may be an advantage.

Take the example of Christine Day, the former CEO of the clothing company Lululemon and former co-president of Starbucks. There's no doubt that she was already a very astute businesswoman, but her experience in women's active wear was limited when she took on the CEO role at Lululemon. And yet, her experience at Lululemon was an extraordinary success, viewed through both the lens of the analysts and that of her employees.

Transformational Leadership

There are many different models of leadership. There's the oft-quoted Situational Leadership Model, which prescribes a different level of leadership depending on the maturity of the team members. There is Kurt Lewin's Change Management Model, which argues that there are three different styles of leadership: autocratic, democratic and laissez-faire. There's the Goleman,

Boyatzis and McKee Model of Emotional Leadership—and there are many others. (You can read more on these models in the very useful website Mind Tools[22]).

However, is now widely accepted that the concept of transformational leadership is the style to aspire to. Matt Church, in *Amplifiers*, speaks of "the Amplifiers" as having transformational leadership with a focus on results, while building the capability to do even more.[6]

The website Mind Tools has this to say:

> *Leadership style frameworks are all useful in different situations; however, in business "transformational leadership" is often the most effective leadership style to use.*
>
> *Transformational leaders have integrity and high emotional intelligence. They motivate people with a shared vision of the future, and they communicate well. They're also typically self-aware, authentic, empathetic, and humble.*
>
> *Transformational leaders inspire their team members because they expect the best from everyone, and they hold themselves accountable for their actions. They set clear goals, and they have good conflict-resolution skills. This leads to high productivity and engagement.[23]*

Models, theories and the like are helpful. They provide structure and definitions and help provide a mental path. To make the theories more practical and attainable, we will be talking later in the book about how to create your own leadership persona or style.

The Crucibles of Leadership

There's yet another side to this concept of leadership characteristics: "Crucibles", a term coined by Warren Bennis and Robert Thomas. According to Bennis and Thomas, leaders can often emerge through tragedy or extreme hardship or some other "transformative experience through which an individual comes to a new or an altered sense of identity."[24]

Dr Margot Wood an expert on leadership and organisational effectiveness, shares her insights into the attributes of leaders who've had a crucible experience:

- Whilst many did fail, they learnt from the failure. In itself failure can be a transformative experience and what may look like failure (at one point) can in fact be seen entirely differently from a later perspective. Many 'failures' in terms of strategies, decisions etc., that just needed time for the true impact to be revealed.

- They jumped into something that was beyond what they thought they were capable of doing.

- They had both meaning and purpose (or "deep smarts"). [25]

There's probably no better example of the Crucibles of Leadership than the story of Emily and Rick Parish, whose four-year-old son died from brain cancer. Their response to this tragedy was to set up the Telethon Adventurers—a not-for-profit dedicated to finding the cure for childhood cancers. Since 2012 they've raised millions of dollars, brought together experts from all over the world and galvanised a community and are now widely considered to be leading the way in fundraising for research into childhood brain cancer.

Another example—Sonja Cox, the 2013 WA Telstra Business Woman of the Year, went through a series of personal crucible experiences to emerge as a leader in the corrective services within Western Australia. You can read more about her story on the website, but the experience of her boyfriend being murdered when she was 18 set the path for her extraordinary career in corrective services, and was one of her crucible experiences. [26]

Power: The Dark Side of Leadership

Writer Justin Locke has written a wonderful essay on the dark side of leadership. In it he states: "Power is seductive, it is addictive, it is delicious, and when you get power, remaining objective and keeping your wits about you is not easy."[27]

No doubt we've all seen leaders who have let power go to their heads. Their behaviour becomes reckless and has very little to do with the people they're meant to serve; it becomes all about making the most of the perceived power that comes from their position. And then there are those that exercise leadership in very dark ways – think of Hitler; no doubt a charismatic leader to begin with, before the power took over.

Going back to the definitions of a great leader— and how great leadership comes from your behaviour rather than your position— it's easy to see how such people have positional power but aren't great leaders. It's a common mistake to misuse power, particularly from those new to the leadership game. Don't fall for it. You are smarter than that.

TAKE A MOMENT $\cdots\cdots\cdots\cdots\cdots\cdots\cdots\cdots\cdots\cdots\cdots\cdots\cdots\cdots$

Think about the characteristics of leaders you have worked with, both good and less so. What characteristics did they possess? Now, take a moment to think about the impact that these characteristics had on you and your team. What workarounds did you create to counter them? How would you say that this impacted on the performance of the team?

STICKY MESSAGES :: A VERY SHORT RECAP

- Good leaders generally display the same set of characteristics.

- Transformational leadership is widely considered to be the most important and effective of all leadership styles.

- If you are not naturally charismatic, don't panic.

- While intellect, curiosity and business acumen will always be helpful for any leader, there's no need to have a deep expertise in the area in which you are leading.

- Through appalling hardship and tragedy, the most extraordinary of leaders often emerge.

- Power can be addictive and tantalising.

RESOURCES

There are plenty of great resources on www.dowhatyousay.com.au including a link to my interview with Sonja Cox. There is also the essay from Justin Locke on the dark side of power and some articles on whether your boss is a psychopath! Finally, a link to the wonderful Brené Brown's site which has a wonderful manifesto on leadership.

PART 2
Ten Tools to Give You the Courage to Lead

Tool #1: Do What You Say You'll Do

You are what you do, not what you say you'll do.

—C.G. Jung

This first tool is probably the simplest to describe. When I interviewed Brian Cook, the CEO of the Geelong Football Club, I asked him if there was one thing that emerging leaders could do that would make a difference to the way they lead. His answer was as simple as it was powerful:

Do What You Say You'll Do[1].

Sounds obvious, yes?

There are several reasons why this is so important. It builds your credibility with your team and the wider organisation and stakeholders. Even more importantly, it builds trust, of which credibility is a component. We'll go into building trust in more detail in a later section, but as an entrée to it, the CIPD/ University of Bath report *Experiencing Trustworthy Leadership* has this to say:

> What matters in generating trust amongst
> followers are the everyday actions and behaviours
> of leaders that demonstrate their essential ability,

benevolence, integrity and predictability— drivers of trustworthiness. People do not gauge trustworthiness on the basis of what they are told about the individual competence of a leader— they gauge trustworthiness on ... that person's leadership actions and practice in the workplace...[28]

TAKE A MOMENT

Think about the leaders discussed in the previous sections. Think about the ones who were great, and the ones who were not so great. For the ones who came up on the negative side of the scale, it's likely that a lack of trust or credibility was somewhere in the mix.

Think about how your team or stakeholders perceive you at present. Would they say that you deliver on your promises? Would they say that you get back to them with answers? Would they say that you "Do What You Say You'll Do"? And if the answer to those questions is no, then consider why. Is it forgetfulness? Is it not knowing the right answers? Is it not wanting to offend or upset someone? Or are there factors outside your control, and you use that as an excuse for not going back to the person you've made a promise to?

I've laboured the point a bit because this is *such* a vital tool.

And it's something that every single one of us can learn and implement immediately, irrespective of our innate personality style and characteristics.

Implementing: Do What You Say You'll Do

Doing what you say you are going to do *does not* mean giving everyone what he or she wants or agreeing with what everyone says. Of course, there will be times when it's impossible to give people what they want. Employees might want information on whether the company is being sold, and even if you are privy to that information, you cannot share it. There may be times when employees want you to investigate the possibility of a pay rise and the answer comes back as "no".

Doing what you say you are going to do *does not* preclude such situations. It simply means that you have a way to deal with them that doesn't break the trust and confidence of your team in you.

Here are four steps you can take to Do What You Say You'll Do:

1. Be very careful about what you actually commit to doing. As already discussed, there will be things that you simply won't be able to do, despite your absolute best intentions. Be mindful of this. Can you only commit to being able to ask a question on behalf of the person? If so, tell the person that this is what you will do. Make sure that, as far as possible, you only commit to doing things that you have a good chance of delivering on. If you know you aren't going to be able to deliver, *do not* commit to doing it!

2. Check the understanding with the person: what did they "hear" that you would do, and by when?

3. Keep a record of what you promise and to whom. Don't rely on your memory— write it down. What did you say you would do, for whom and by when?

4. Deliver on your commitments. Even if the answer is "I've checked and we're no further forward", it's critical that you come back to the person— proactively, not when they approach you—to update them.

While these four steps may at first seem a little artificial or forced, as with everything they'll become easier with practice.

Saying Sorry and Moving Forward

What about times when you think you'll be able to deliver on something, but the reality is that it isn't possible? In these instances, there's something very powerful about an apology: acknowledge what you said you would do, and acknowledge you didn't (or couldn't) deliver.

Of course, doing this over and over again in itself breaks trust and dilutes credibility, but most people have a built-in "reasonableness" factor—they know when someone genuinely has made a mistake and that it's a one-off, not their general pattern of behaviour.

But what if you have been a serial under-deliverer to your team or stakeholders, for reasons either within your control or not? There are two approaches you can take here, depending on the team and stakeholders, the environment and who you are.

- You can be upfront and say, "I know I've let you down by not delivering, or not doing what I said I would. I want to let you know that from here on it will be different. I need your help to keep me on track and accountable." or

- You can just start doing things differently and let your actions speak louder than words.

The advantage to the first approach is that you're letting people know that you know you could do better, and that you're prepared to give it a go. But if you take this approach, be prepared for people to hold you to account and be harsher if you make mistakes.

The advantage to the second approach is that it's less dramatic—you can just get on and do things without any dramatic proclamations. The disadvantage is that sometimes, despite changing your ways, you can be tarred with your old brush—and people need to know that you've changed, which means being overt about it to some extent.

Which approach you take depends on your reading of the lay of the land, so spend some time thinking about that before you dive in. It also helps for you to think about why you've been under-delivering. If it's because you find giving feedback hard or because you commit to too much, read on—we'll address these issues in a later section.

TAKE A MOMENT

Now, give it a go. Write down all the commitments you've made. Are there things that are outstanding? Are there people you avoid in the corridor because you were meant to get back to them? Write it all down. Then make a plan for how you're going to address what's on the list and how you're going to approach going forward.

And practice. Be prepared that it won't always work out perfectly. Building new approaches to leadership is like building any other new habit, skill or attribute—it takes time and practice, and the ability to be gentle on yourself when it doesn't go according to plan. A little bit of courage won't go astray here either!

STICKY MESSAGES :: A VERY SHORT RECAP

- Doing what you say you are going to do builds trust and credibility with your team or stakeholders.

- This doesn't mean always giving people what they want or agreeing with them.

- It does mean being careful and clear about what you commit to, checking understanding, keeping a record and then delivering.

- Even if you've been a serial under-deliverer, this is one tool that it's never too late to start using. Just begin from today and watch what happens.

RESOURCES

There are plenty of great resources on www.dowhatyousay.com.au including the *Experiencing Trustworthy Leadership* report from the Chartered Institute of Personnel and Development (CIPD) and the University of Bath.

Tool # 2: The "Would I Sit on That Toilet?" Test

Would I sit on that bog?

—Jon Allen

While working for the Royal Mail in London, UK, I had the privilege of working with a very wise and clever man, Jon Allen, who had what is possibly the best-titled leadership tool of all time: the "Would I Sit on That Bog?" Test.

This tool is pretty much as it reads. Would I expect my team to do something that I wouldn't be prepared to do? Would I expect them to work in conditions that I wouldn't work in?

As Brian Cook, says,

> *They must have the ability to be as selfless as possible and their leadership is about the people they lead and not about themselves.[1]*

Why Does This Matter?

This is an interesting test, as inevitably the first argument raised is: "Well, I worked hard for my seat on the executive. I deserve my parking space at the front, executive suite facilities and plush toilets. And when they get to this level, then they can have that too."

On the face of it, this might not sound too unreasonable— but think about it for just a moment. It's not really about what you believe you deserve, but more about what you expect your team to put up with.

So, if the thought of using the men's facilities in the production area fills you with horror, then why would you expect them to be okay for your team? If you cringe when you make yourself a cup of coffee in the mess hall, then why is it okay for your team to use this every day? Why is it okay that they work in extreme heat when the air-conditioning breaks down, but you continue to have your office suite suitably chilled?

In general, what message are you sending if you expect your team to work in conditions that you yourself will not?

Herzberg's theory

Some of this is basic psychology. Frederick Herzberg's two-factor theory concludes that certain factors in the workplace result in job satisfaction, but if those factors are absent, they don't lead to dissatisfaction but rather to no satisfaction.

Herzberg distinguished between:

- Motivators (e.g. challenging work, recognition, responsibility) that give positive satisfaction, and

- Hygiene factors (e.g. status, job security, salary and fringe benefits) that don't motivate if present, but if absent result in demotivation.

According to Herzberg, the factors leading to job satisfaction are "separate and distinct from those that lead to job dissatisfaction." The characteristics associated with job dissatisfaction are called hygiene factors. When these have been adequately addressed, people will not be dissatisfied nor will they be satisfied. If you want to motivate your team, you then have to focus on satisfaction factors like achievement, recognition, and responsibility. [29]

The word "hygiene" is used because these factors play a similar role to, for example, basic hygiene in a hospital—it doesn't cure illnesses, but it does protect against them. This fits nicely with the "Would I Sit on that Toilet?" Test. While ensuring that hygiene factors are met won't guarantee motivation and job satisfaction, not having those factors will mean that there's demotivation.

It's Not Just About Doing the Bare Minimum

This isn't about your basic requirement to comply with workplace health and safety laws—this is about what's reasonable and appropriate given the broader context and environment. What message does it send to your team? This is particularly important the further up the organisational ladder you go, as it gets easier and easier to become removed from the reality of your indirect reports.

Here's what I'm not saying about this tool: I'm not saying that all organisations need to treat everyone exactly the same; I'm not saying that you would expect a CEO to operate out of an open-space cubicle, although plenty do this. I'm not saying that you'd expect a sales director to wear a uniform—although again, plenty do.

What *I am* saying is that if you expect your team to work in conditions that you find intolerable, then without doubt they are forming a negative perception of you and your leadership approach. And if the issues are being raised over and over again, only for you to ignore or dismiss them, then this will no doubt be eroding confidence in you as a leader.

Think of terms like ivory tower, out of touch, unreachable, disconnected. You might not think it matters if these are applied to you, until you recall the characteristics of the great leaders we've discussed—those terms aren't usually ascribed to great leaders. Think of the example of Arthur T. Demoulas and the grocery store. His employees were prepared to sacrifice pay for him because they were connected—he wasn't in an ivory tower.

Another of the people I had the great privilege of interviewing for this book was Dr Penny Flett. She is the CEO of the Brightwater Care Group, a recipient of an Order of Australia and a Centenary Medal, a finalist in the Australian of the Year Awards, the 1998 Telstra Australian Business Woman of the Year—and the list goes on.

We talked about the significant changes she had implemented within Brightwater and I asked her how she'd managed to bring her staff on the journey, given the traditionally low pay and hard work that the care industry is known for. In probing further, I think the answer to this question is largely about Penny's extraordinary leadership skills. She has managed to build an organisation where it is clear that she cares and that her leadership team cares.

Penny told me a story about how whenever she goes to visit the Brightwater laundry facility, there's a squeal of delight from the laundry staff when they realise she's there, and she always gets lots of hugs. "We are all in the same place together," she told me. [30]

The message I take from this is that if you can be a CEO with every conceivable accolade and still be humble, still care about your staff, still care what conditions they work in, then surely the rest of us can do that too.

Leading from the Front

Another example I have is of a leader was very senior in the organisation and showed extraordinary leadership in the "go live" phase of an important organisational project. He was there, night after night, weekend after weekend, working alongside the project team. He would be the one that sent the others home when he could see that they were getting too tired, who would bring in healthy food and who made sure the thank you and rewards were handed out soon after the project was completed. There was no sense that it was "do as I say, not do as I do"; he was there, working side by side. The positive perception of him and his leadership lasted long after the end of the project. Contrast this with another senior leader in the organisation, who popped in once or twice, who didn't know the names of the project team and for whom it was very much a superficial approach to leading from the front.

TAKE A MOMENT

Think about the conditions that your team work under, and whether you would work under these conditions. If not, then ask yourself if they are reasonable. Have there been ongoing complaints about the condition of the toilets and the tearoom? What could you do immediately to address this issue, and what will take a longer-term plan?

STICKY MESSAGES :: A VERY SHORT RECAP

- "Would I Sit on that Toilet?" is not about treating everyone the same, but rather about being reasonable in how you treat people and what conditions you expect them to operate under.

- If basic hygiene factors aren't being met, don't expect motivated, engaged employees.

RESOURCES

There are plenty of great resources on www.dowhatyousay.com.au that are worth a look.

Tool #3: Communicate, Communicate, Communicate

The single biggest problem in communication is the illusion that it has taken place.

—George Bernard Shaw

Groan. Communication. *Yes, yes,* I hear you say, *I know all about this. I do communicate.* You may even be tempted to skip this section. But I urge you not to. Why? Well, the thing about every single one of the tools I'm sharing with you in this book is that they require you to communicate effectively.

Now, in some people's minds this might mean giving a rousing speech and inspiring the troops. But that isn't what I'm talking about. I am talking about the very essence of communication—to send a message and for that message to be received as intended.

It's the latter part of this definition that almost always gets forgotten. We think that because we've sent a message (however it's done), we have communicated—and then we get frustrated and wonder why, *still*, the recipient doesn't get it. Your job as a communicator isn't done until the message has been received and understood as you intended.

Research from expert change management organisation PROSCI® shows that a person needs to hear a message five to seven times before they actually take it in.[31] Seven times … think about how often we communicate a message—sometimes a really important message—via email or memo, and then fail to check whether it was received or opened, let alone understood.

The Five Steps to Great Communication

1. What is the message that you're trying to convey, including any required actions?

2. How important is this message?

3. Who is the message going to?

4. What medium are you using to communicate it, and is this the right medium for this message and this recipient?

5. How will you check that the message has been received and understood? Do you need to reinforce it in some other way?

If the message is very important, either to you or the recipient, and you are emailing it, ask yourself why. Can there be a face-to-face discussion or phone call first? So many misunderstandings and conflicts occur because the recipient was unable either to check or to understand an email, a social media message or a text. Research by Daniel Goleman shows that emails written in a positive tone are often received neutrally and emails written in a neutral tone are often received negatively. With important messages, do you really want to be adding a layer of unintended emotion?[32]

If It's So Simple, Why Don't People Communicate Effectively?

I believe there are three main reasons why people avoid effective communication, despite knowing how to do it.

1. A difficult message. Of course, many people prefer to email difficult messages—it seems so much easier than having the conversation face to face or over the phone. Unfortunately, this will often make communication harder in the long term. Yes, some messages are very difficult to deliver, but often we make these conversations out to be bigger and more difficult in our minds, and so either don't have the conversation or do it ineffectively via electronic means. We'll talk more about giving feedback in a later section.

2. It's not my job. Research shows that the person an employee wants to hear a message from largely depends on the nature of the message. For those about strategy, change and longer-term issues, employees want to hear from a senior leader. For those relating to personal implications, employees want to hear from their direct manager.[33]

3. Fear of speaking in front of groups. There's an oft-quoted statistic that people's number one fear is public speaking, with death coming in at number two and the dentist at number three. There is something about having to get up in front of a crowd that can make even the most articulate one-on-one communicator go to pieces.

David Koutsoukis is a leadership and team development specialist who is also the past president of the National Speakers Association of Australia. I asked him for some tips on how to overcome stage fright and speak well. He shares his tips below:

> *Public speaking is an important skill for leaders that comes naturally for some and terrifies others. How well we speak impacts what people think of us as a leader so it is important that we do it well. The good news is that there are some simple principles you can apply to become a more effective speaker.*
>
> *There are literally hundreds of techniques and tactics to engage and influence an audience. In time, you might like to learn, practice and implement some of these, but there are three key principles you need to know that will help you become an effective speaker and influential leader.*
>
> *Aristotle studied the speaking patterns of the great orators of his time and was fascinated by the fact that some speakers had their audience hanging off every word, while others were virtually ignored. He noticed three common patterns used by these effective speakers [that] he labelled Logos, Pathos and Ethos. In time they have become known as the three Modes of Persuasion, or Aristotle's three appeals.*
>
> ***Ethos**—an appeal to the audience's need for trust. When they see a speaker, people subconsciously ask themselves "Does this person have good character, are they reliable and trustworthy, should I respect their*

opinion?" Ethos is the root word of ethics. Examples of Ethos in a speech include demonstrating ethical behaviour, using respect when talking about others, showing humility and telling personal stories that illustrate good character. Ethos will also be judged by your actions "off the stage". People will make assumptions about your character by your everyday behaviour. Demonstrate Ethos and people will be more likely to listen to you.

Logos *is an appeal to the audience's need for logic. People subconsciously ask themselves "Does this person makes sense, do they have evidence to back up their key points, do they present a logical argument?" Logos is the root word of logic. Examples of Logos include presenting your speech in an organised, well-structured manner, using real-life examples, and the use of analytical information such as statistics, facts and other evidence to support an argument. Demonstrate Logos and people will be more likely to be persuaded by you.*

Pathos*—an appeal to the audience's need for emotional connection. People subconsciously ask themselves "Does this person connect with me emotionally, do they get me excited or agitated, am I motivated enough to take action?" Pathos is the root word of empathy—the ability to share the emotions of others. Examples of Pathos in a speech include showing emotions like joy, anger, sadness, surprise, optimism, love and awe. You can also stimulate emotions through techniques such* *as stories, analogies and metaphors, surprise, visuals and humour. Demonstrate Pathos and people will be more likely to be motivated to action by you.*

As a leader you don't need to be a polished professional speaker to motivate and influence others. As long as you demonstrate Logos, Pathos and Ethos you will connect with your people and motivate them to action.

No News

The last point on communication is that no news is still news and still needs to be communicated. As discussed earlier, if you've promised to get back to someone but haven't because there's been no movement on the issue: tell them that there is "no news", as well as what you're doing about it (if anything). The very act of doing this will build trust rather than erode it.

TAKE A MOMENT

Think about good leaders you've worked with or heard about. What was their communication style? What did they do that was special? What could you learn from them? Write down one aspect of communication that you could do differently right from this moment.

STICKY MESSAGES :: A VERY SHORT RECAP

- Communication is important because every single tool that we talk about requires that you're able to communicate.
- Research shows that employees need to hear a message seven times before it truly sinks in. This is particularly true of important or more complex messages.
- There are five steps to great communication.
- There are generally three reasons why people avoid communicating: fear of speaking in public, fear of what the other person is going to say, and a belief it's not their job.
- When speaking in public, think of David Koutsoukis' Ethos, Logos and Pathos: credibility, logic and emotion.
- No news is still news!

RESOURCES

There are plenty of great resources on www.dowhatyousay.com.au including some great tips on how to communicate really well and David Koutsoukis' 21 tips on better public speaking.

Tool #4: Build a Great Team

None of us is as smart as all of us.

—Kenneth H. Blanchard

Sometimes a technical expert is promoted into a leadership position because they are extremely good at the technical aspect of the work. This leads to two problems: firstly, they're often not equipped to lead the team from a leadership perspective; and secondly, they often find it very hard to let go of their old job and start doing their new one. They try to keep doing what they used to do in addition to what they now think they're meant to be doing, and end up doing neither particularly well.

Does this sound like you?

The key to this dilemma is to have the right team around you. You should be clear on what the team is meant to be doing and what each team member brings, not only from a skills perspective but also from a personality and behavioural perspective.

Dr Fiona Wood, esteemed burns surgeon, 2003 recipient of the Order of Australia, and 2005 Australian of the Year sums this up beautifully in our interview when she says:

Respect what the members of the team bring together. Think of yourself as a conductor of an orchestra. The first violin has skills that are essential and different to the second violin, etc.[34]

New Leader's Team Audit

Of course, often you inherit your team and don't have the luxury of creating a new one from scratch. But even so, you can do the following:

- Do you know the purpose of your team and how this directly fits with the broader organisational mission, vision and strategy? If not, then find out.

- Do you know not just what your team is expected to produce, but also what additional value they're expected to bring to the organisation?

Now, think about your team:

- Who is in your team?

  - What is their role? What are they expected to deliver?

  - What is their education and background? What work and life experience do they bring?

  - What special skills do they bring to the team? This might not be about their technical expertise, but rather something unique: perhaps they are particularly good at organising social events or have outstanding customer service skills.

- Has there been 360-degree feedback or personality or other profiling done of the team that you can review? 360-degree feedback is a survey where a 360 degree sweep of feedback is sought and then compiled and analysed. Usually this means from a manager, peers and direct and indirect reports. It can also include customers and suppliers.

If you don't know the answers to these questions, work them out. And if it isn't feasible to start the team from scratch or significantly add to it, think carefully about the mix of skills and personalities. What do you have? What are you missing?

You may be tempted to recruit only your favourite type of people, but the key here is balance. I once worked with a team that had seven out of eight members with the same thinking style, which was all about process and structure. That left the team very exposed in terms of thinking around people, around strategy, around blue-sky ideas.

Another temptation may be to recruit or keep people in positions because you perceive them as less talented than you. Almost always, though, great leaders will say that they succeed because of the fantastic people around them. Remember that you are only as good as the weakest link in your team. When I interviewed Dr Penny Flett, she was clear that one of the reasons for her success was her team:

> *They could do without me for a period of time, but I couldn't do without them.*[30]

Getting to Know One Another

Another team I worked with had been working together for years and yet couldn't tell me the first thing about one another. They didn't know who their colleagues were outside of work, what was important to them as people, what their lives looked like. All they knew was what they brought to the team while at work. By the end of one-hour interviews with each of them, I knew more about them as people than their colleagues did. How? By asking the right questions and being interested in the answers.

Perhaps it sounds obvious, but the first step to building any new team is getting to know one another. It's vital for building trust. In Patrick Lencioni's classic book *The Five Dysfunctions of a Team*, trust is the basis for great team performance.[35]

Lencioni's book is well worth a read, as it illustrates the point that it's hard to get true high performance from your team without really knowing them first.

If your organisation has an HR department, talk to them about what assistance they can offer in terms of getting to know your team. They may have a profiling tool to assess your team members or suggestions for team-building exercises that you can run during your meetings. They may also be able to run programmes that illustrate how different people think, and how you can use this knowledge to avoid misunderstandings.

But even without assistance from HR, there are very simple things you can do. Think about building in opportunities for social engagement within the team. Bear in mind that not everyone is happy to give up their evenings or weekends to do this, so look for opportunities (both structured and unstructured) during the workday to begin with. Also, respect that different people wish to share things to varying degrees.

You should also look for opportunities to have one-on-one time with your team outside of the work environment (out in the field, for example) and actively ask questions that will help you get to know everyone better.

One leader that I work with is running team building and getting-to-know-you exercises during each monthly meeting. Team members share responsibility for finding and running the exercises each month.

Stages of Team Formation

One other thing to remember is that no team will perform perfectly from the beginning. All teams go through stages of development.

Bruce Tuckman famously designed a model showing that teams go through four stages: forming, storming, norming and performing.[36] It's important to recognise which stage the team is in before moving forward through the stages to performance. This is another issue to discuss with your HR department, as they should be able to provide you with tools to recognise and move from stage to stage. If you don't have HR in your organisation, there are online tools you can use to give you an idea of what stage your team is at.

Your Role Within the Team

Finally, be clear on your own role. Go back to the role of the leader:

- Set and communicate direction.

- Align individuals and groups of people to a common purpose.

- Role model and communicate agreed values.

- Demonstrate self-development and growing others.

- Ensure individual team member's authenticity and integrity.

- Hold team members to be accountable to themselves and the team.

You'll notice that there isn't much in there about actually *doing the work*. Of course, that's part of any job. But your job as a leader is predominantly to lead.

A major element of this is the concept of growing others. One of the keys to building a great team is for every member to have their strengths maximised, and your job is to recognise strengths and develop them on an individual basis. There are many wonderful tools available these days, often either free or relatively inexpensive, which will help you do this.

Remember that development isn't the same as training. In fact, good development is 70 per cent on-the-job experienced based practice and growth (think new projects, challenging work, etc.), 20 per cent coaching, mentoring and development through other people and 10 per cent formal learning interventions. This is great news for leaders: development can mean a great return for relatively little dollar investment. However it also means that you need to know your team, what they're meant to deliver, and how to bring out the best in each of them by empowering them and giving them access to challenging work or other forms of development.

TAKE A MOMENT

Have you done your team audit? If not, do it now. Then think back to what the team is expected to deliver. Is it clear how these particular people can achieve this? How can you maximise your team's special gifts and strengths? And are you clear on what you need to deliver? Are there gaps in what needs to be done? What can you do to start building trust?

RESOURCES

There are plenty of great resources on www.dowhatyousay.com.au including some information on how different people think, and how you can use this to your advantage.

STICKY MESSAGES :: A VERY SHORT RECAP

- Do you know your team? Have you done the team audit?

- Different people bring different skills, behaviours and thinking styles to the team. You need a balance, not clones!

- Recruit people who bring more to the team, not less.

- Trust is paramount.

- All teams go through different stages of development. This is normal and expected. Know where your team is and how to move it to the next stage.

- Are you clear on what your role is within the team?

- What can you do to develop your team? Remember the 70:20:10 rule.

- Get help if you need it.

Tool #5: Learn to Embrace Conflict Within Teams

Deal with it, or let it go.

—*Rob Whitechurch*

Conflict is a natural dynamic in any healthy relationship. So the presence of conflict isn't the issue, but rather how that conflict is addressed—or not addressed! This is particularly true of teams— as there are often additional dynamics such as organisational politics at play.

According to Patrick Lencioni's *The Five Dysfunctions of a Team*:

> *Teams that engage in productive conflict know that the only purpose is to produce the best possible solution in the shortest period of time. They discuss and resolve issues more quickly and completely than others and they emerge from heated debates with no residual feelings or collateral damage …*
>
> *Contrary to the notion that teams waste time and energy arguing, those that avoid conflict actually doom themselves to revisiting issues again and again. They often ask team members to take issues "off line" which seems to be a euphemism for avoiding dealing with an important topic.[35]*

If only it were that easy!

Three Simple Techniques to Deal with Conflict

I asked Rob Whitechurch, a leadership expert, for some suggestions on how to manage conflict. He suggested these three techniques:

1. Reframe the Conflict

Wherever there's a team, there's the potential for conflict. It's inevitable. If there is no conflict, there is probably no interdependency between team members—and interdependency is essential for any high-performing team.

So the first technique is to reframe and see conflict as a normal part of any functioning team; it is a healthy sign that issues matter and people care. Also, remember what Bruce Tuckman said of the stages of team development: is the conflict simply part of the team working their way through the "storming" stage, or is it something more?

2. Deal With It or Let It Go

The second technique is so simple and yet so powerful:

Choice	Action	Health
Confront	Deal with it	✓
Let Go	Drop It	✓
Leave	Avoid It	✗
Go Underground	Carry it	✗ ✗ ✗

The first two options are the healthy approaches to conflict management. The last two are often the cause of lingering resentment and reduced trust.

The two key components to the technique of "Deal With It or Let It Go" are:

- The 48-Hour Rule: you have 48 hours to deal with it or drop it. That means *really* drop it—"No hands from the grave."

- The team keeps one another accountable.

3. Avoid Triangulation

The third technique is my favourite. There's such a temptation in teams not to address an issue with the person directly, but rather to triangulate by going to another team member and having a whinge. Inevitably this gets back to the source, causing greater conflict and/or reducing trust in the relationship.

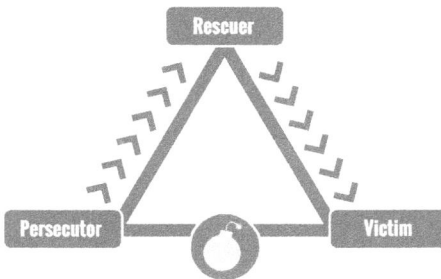

The illustration above shows the triangulation dynamic. The "persecutor" goes to the "rescuer" who then addresses it with the "victim". The language is emotive, but deliberately so. The "rescuer" (usually the manager/leader) is helping to "rescue" the person who has the issue, rather than coaching and supporting them to deal directly with the person with whom they have the issue.

Some leaders use triangulation to "divide and conquer" and believe that it illustrates the power they have, but in reality the reverse is true. It may work to begin with, but your team will quickly realise that you're doing it with everyone and trust will be diluted.

The good news is that this one is easy to deal with. Again, it's about the team holding one another to account. If a team member comes to you and whinges about a colleague, the first thing you should ask is: "Have you had a conversation with them about this?" If the answer is "no", then by all means provide coaching around how to frame that conversation, but don't allow yourself to become part of the drama.

TAKE A MOMENT

Think about how your team deals with conflict. Could you use any of the three techniques above to make a difference? How would you go about doing this? Do you need assistance from HR or from an external facilitator to draw the issues out? If you don't have HR at your organisation, what other resources can you use?

STICKY MESSAGES :: A VERY SHORT RECAP

- Conflict doesn't have to be bad. Know your conflict and deal with it accordingly.

- Try the three techniques for dealing with conflict within your team:

  1. Reframe it.

  2. Deal with it or let it go.

  3. Don't allow triangulation.

- If in doubt, seek help!

RESOURCES

There are plenty of great resources on www.dowhatyousay.com.au that are worth a look, including more detail on the "Deal With It or Let It Go" technique.

Tool # 6 Feedback: Right Place, Right Time, Right Way

We all need people who will give us feedback. That's how we improve.

—Bill Gates

I can see you rolling your eyes already. I think that giving feedback might be up there with public speaking as an area of leadership that people really, really don't like—and often will do anything to avoid.

And yet, how can any of us know how we're doing unless someone gives us feedback? Good, bad or indifferent, it's good to know that we're making progress—or not. Otherwise we keep on keeping on. There are so many examples I've seen over the years of employees who have complained that "if only" they'd been told there was something wrong, they would or could have done something differently. Instead, these cases are stored up and then presented as a *fait accompli* at the end-of-year performance review, when it's often too late.

Great leaders actively seek out feedback and they give great feedback. Here's another excerpt from my interview with Brian Cook:

I have four or five really close friends that I have had for 30 years and we do lunch every six months to get feedback on how they see that I am going. They are brutally honest.[1]

Feedback is a tool that builds on and contributes to other tools—you need to be able to communicate to give feedback and you need to be able to give feedback in order to do other things, such as be a good coach (which we'll address as another tool later in this section of the book).

Think about when you have had to receive feedback from someone and they have been sitting across the table from you. Think about the barrier that that table put in the way. Leadership and HR consultant Jaine Edge, has this to say in her blog on effective communication:

… I used to work for a CEO who had a huge old desk, a big and very tall chair behind it and then two very low visitor chairs in front. It was a really intimidating set up and I think designed to do just that. It felt very much like visiting the principal as a primary school pupil.[37]

Contrast that with Brené Brown's wonderful take on feedback in her book *Daring Greatly* (which is worth reading for that section alone). She makes the point that giving feedback is about "sitting on the same side of the table."[38] Rather than feedback being used as a tool to punish, it is about genuinely helping the person to grow and move forward. Personally, I think there is nothing sadder than someone realising that they have been doing the same thing throughout their whole career, and no one has ever had the courage to tell them and work with them to change it.

One other perspective is that of Seth Godin, who explains the fear of giving feedback by linking it back to the "fight or flight" mechanism of the brain. In *Linchpin*, he writes:

> *Why is it that so many bosses shy away from useful criticism or substantive leadership? Why is it so easy to hide behind an office door or a title instead of looking people in the eye and making a difference? Same answer. The amygdala resists looking people in the eye, because doing so is threatening and exposes it to risk ... In fact, if we go down the list of behaviors that are highly valued because of their scarcity, almost all of them are related to bringing a conscious and generous mind to the work, instead of indulging our lizard brain's reflexes of fear, revenge and conquest.*[2]

Five Tips on Giving Feedback

1. Make it timely. It's no good saying, weeks after the event, "Remember when you did …" Even if the employee remembers the event, the impact has gone—and there's also the residual feeling of "Why hasn't this been raised with me until now?" which means this becomes yet another example of reducing trust.

2. Think about what you're hoping to achieve from the feedback. Do you just want to vent because you've had a bad day and the person has done something that set you off? What specific message do you want to give? What do you want to occur as a result of the feedback—what specific behavioural change or action?

3. Ask for permission to proceed. Check in with the person: "Is now a good time to give you some feedback?" If the person is in the middle of a work or personal crisis, then even with the best delivery in the world, it's unlikely that your feedback will be received and taken on board.

4. If you're uncomfortable with providing feedback, use a tool such as AID: Action, Impact and Desired Behaviour. That is, what was the action or the incident that you are giving feedback on, what was the impact on the other person of that action/incident, and what would be a better or more desirable way of approaching the action or an alterative way or a different way going forward? It may feel artificial at first, but it gives a useful script, and over time it will become easier and more natural to use.

ACTION

IMPACT

DESIRED BEHAVIOUR

5. Remember that feedback isn't just about the negative. Positive feedback is equally powerful, but always be specific about what was good, and why and what the impact of that will be. You can use the AID tool equally well for both positive and negative feedback.

What Not to Do

- Ignore an issue and hope it will get better—and then store it up with a number of other issues to present all at once.

- Do it in public. As Justin Langer, the coach of the Western Australia Cricket Team, says: "Praise publicly and criticise in private."[39]

- Blame the system. You can provide really effective feedback any time, irrespective of what the formal performance management timeline or process says.

- Own the feedback. Don't say, "I've been told to tell you." Don't pass the buck.

- Feel like you have to be "tough" and aggressive. Quietly assertive will get you a lot further than aggressive. If you don't know how to do assertive, you should get some help, practice with a script and learn.

- Ignore it because you're worried that the person will get angry, not like you anymore, bitch about you behind your back or retaliate with his or her own list.

Giving Feedback to Your Mates

It's really hard giving feedback to people who were your mates before you took over the role of team leader. The only way around this is to acknowledge the elephant in the room: "I know this might feel weird, but … " Be assertive, not passive or aggressive. Speak your truth quietly and with respect.

Do not, do not, *do not* ignore it and hope it will go away or get better, or that they'll move to another team and you won't have to deal with it. You're the leader of the team and this is part of your job! This is one of the bits of the job that is going to require a bit of courage.

Receiving Feedback

There's another side to this feedback coin—you should not just be open to receiving feedback, but also positively encourage it. Often organisations will facilitate this by conducting 360-degree feedback surveys, and of course performance reviews are meant to provide you with good feedback. But as a leader, you can do so much more to model this yourself.

Actively seek feedback from your team, your peers, your customers and your boss. Don't wait for formal processes. One leader I know has a formal agenda he uses each week with his team. He asks: "What feedback do you have for me? What can I do differently, better? What would you like me to stop doing, start doing, continue doing?" Remember that how you ask the question makes a difference. If you ask a closed question such as "Do you have any feedback for me?" you're likely to elicit a closed response—almost always "no", as it's scary giving feedback to your boss! Another leader I know asked me to survey his peers and customers formally, asking for what he did well and what he could improve on.

Think about how you receive feedback. This is almost always a case of "actions speak louder than words". If you profess to want to receive feedback, but then spend hours sulking about it, that's not going to encourage people to give you more feedback.

Remember that even though "feedback is a gift" it's simply another person's perception of you or your actions. It doesn't define you, and there may well be times where upon reflection you choose to disagree with it. The key here is to respond rather than react: listen, reflect and then choose your response.

When in doubt, use Brian Cook's methodology on giving feedback as he shared with me in our interview:

Right time, right place, right way.[1]

TAKE A MOMENT

Think about how your team deals with conflict. Could you use any of the three techniques above to make a difference? How would you go about doing this? Do you need assistance from HR or from an external facilitator to draw the issues out? If you don't have HR at your organisation, what other resources can you use?

STICKY MESSAGES :: A VERY SHORT RECAP

- Feedback is a gift.
- Giving feedback may feel unnatural at first, but a tool such as AID can provide structure to the conversation.
- Giving feedback to a friend may be difficult at first, but use the tools in this section to provide structure and practice if need be.
- Receiving feedback is as important as giving feedback.
- Read Brené Brown's manifesto.

RESOURCES

There are plenty of great resources on www. dowhatyousay.com.au including an interview between James Lush and Justin Langer, which is well worth watching; Brené Brown's manifesto on feedback and one of my articles on the five tips to making workplace conversations the best that they can be.

Tool # 7: Learn How to Coach

I never cease to be amazed at the power of the coaching process to draw out the skills or talent that was previously hidden within an individual, and which invariably finds a way to solve a problem previously thought unsolvable.

—*John Russell*

Coaching is a word that's frequently misused. Often we talk about a coach when we mean a mentor—but coaching isn't mentoring; we'll talk later in the book about mentoring.

Max Landsberg's *The Tao of Coaching* describes coaching as follows:

> *Coaching aims to enhance the performance and learning ability of others. It involves giving feedback, but it also includes other techniques such as motivation and effective questioning. And for a manager-coach it includes recognising the coachee's readiness to undertake a particular task, in terms of both their will and skill. Overall, the coach is aiming for the coachee to help her or himself. And as it is a dynamic interaction—it does not rely on a one-way flow of telling or instruction.*[40]

Coaching builds on other tools—communication and feedback—and it's a tool that you can use in a variety of ways throughout life, including in community settings such as sporting clubs, and in family situations.

Ultimately, coaching is about enabling the coachee to come to their own solution around an issue or problem, or an aspect of their development. The coach provides the structure and safe place for the coachee to reach their own answers.

This means that "I think you should do this" isn't coaching; nor is "Here's the way you do it." Those are examples of instructing. There may be times where giving instruction is necessary, but when it's about an issue that someone is grappling with—trying to grow, develop or solve, rather than do—then coaching rather than instructing is necessary.

And here's the thing. Although there may be times when you're able to suggest a solution that the coachee hasn't thought of, the coachee almost always has the answers—and often those answers are so powerful in their simplicity that they are stunning. Dr Penny Flett again:

> *I don't tell people what to do; I enable them to work it out.*[30]

Hang on a Second, How Is This Relevant to Leadership?

We don't often think of coaching as a leadership skill, but when you read about the perspective of Christine Day, the former CEO of Lululemon, you can see that leadership is very much about giving people the space to find their own answers. Day had this to say in a CNNMoney interview about her transformation to being a leader:

> *I was a very bright, smart executive. But I think I majored in being right.*
>
> *The advice that he gave me was [this:] when I was trying to get other people to have ownership or engagement, it wasn't about the telling, it was about other people com[ing] into the idea, and being purpose led and creating the space for others to perform.*
>
> *Once I shifted my leadership into that—creating jobs that are big enough for people is what he called it— that was so powerful for me to shift from having the best idea or problem solving into actually being the best leader of people.[41]*

Or as Maggie Dent says,

> *I believe that exceptional leaders are always committed to creating more leaders than focusing on maintaining one's own place of leadership. Being able to mentor and guide others to grow both personally and professionally and then to step forward has been something that I have strived for even from my earliest days as a teacher.[3]*

A Technique for Coaching

The most popular tool for coaching is the GROW Model:

- What is the Goal of the coachee?

- What is the Reality of the situation at present?

- What Options are there to bridge the gap between reality and the goal?

- What will you do/Wrap up: what specific actions will the coachee commit to make the goal a reality?

Landsberg's *The Tao of Coaching* is a quick and easy read, and illustrates the GROW Model well.[40]

The keys to effective coaching are:

- Listen: that is, *really* listen—don't already be generating a response in your head.

- Play what the coachee is saying back to them, then paraphrase to check your understanding if necessary.

- Ask good, thoughtful questions. If in doubt, go for why, what, how, who, why.

- Coaching can definitely happen on the fly, but it can be so much more effective when there's the time and space set aside for it.

- It probably goes without saying, but coaching is unlike feedback—it requires that the coachee not only wants to be coached but also is ready to be coached. It's impossible to coach effectively if the coachee has been told they *have* to be there.

- Coaching requires an underlying relationship based on trust.

- Coaching requires generosity on behalf of the coach—generosity of time and spirit.

TAKE A MOMENT ···

Think of how you can apply this tool to your leadership. Are you currently coaching someone? Would you benefit from reading The Tao of Coaching?

Can you now see how coaching is different to providing feedback?

If you were to be coached, is there a specific issue you would like to address? What mechanism could you use internally or externally to find a coach?

STICKY MESSAGES :: A VERY SHORT RECAP

- Coaching is different to mentoring and providing feedback.

- Coaching is not instructing or telling—it's about providing the structure and space for the coachee to find their own answers.

- The GROW Model is a simple but effective tool to use when coaching.

- Ask good questions and listen, checking understanding as necessary.

- A good coaching relationship is based on trust.

RESOURCES

There are plenty of great resources on www.dowhatyousay.com.au including some short videos on the GROW Model.

Tool #8: Motivating Your Team: "I Have a Dream"

People often say that motivation doesn't last. Well, neither does bathing – that's why we recommend it daily.

—Zig Ziglar

When we talk about motivation, people's thoughts often turn to big rah-rah speeches that rally the troops. You might be thinking of Martin Luther King Jr.'s *"I Have a Dream"* speech[42] or other inspirational speeches that inspire and motivate—those speeches are incredible and have stood the test of time for a reason.

But the good news is that this isn't generally what motivation is all about. Here we'll talk about the four elements that are key to motivating employees.

1. Start with "Why"

Simon Sinek gave a famous TED Talk on how great leaders start with "why". Why are you doing the work that you are doing? What is the higher purpose of the work? Good leaders make sure that their team members are crystal clear on why they're doing the work. The "how" and the "what" come after that.[43]

If employees know why they're doing the work and why it's important, this gives purpose to the work. And purpose is highly motivating.

2. Alignment of Culture

According to 5 time AFL premiership CEO Brian Cook:

> *I believe good leaders align people around shared missions and values. They empower people to lead and serve other stakeholders. A mission statement is the start of a great strategy that sets an organisational agenda, and a structure and template to build around. For us, the Mission and Values describe "the Geelong Way" from which we build our entire organisation. Every employee should know how they fit and contribute to the mission.*
>
> *…*
>
> *You must decide on what your values should be. It must be an inclusive process. Ask your people what behaviours, if consistently shown, would mean outstanding success for the organisation, define them and place a title on them. For example: team, integrity, excellence, precision, etc. Recruit for these values, reward the demonstration of these values, promote people with these values, place these values into performance reviews.[1]*

As a leader this is all about ensuring, as much as possible, that you and your team live and breathe the organisational values, and are contributing to the organisational mission.

There's nothing worse than a leader who espouses the organisational values (or uses them to describe how others are not performing) but who doesn't live them him or herself.

Culture can be described as "how we do things around here" and is the marriage of the stated (the mission, values, organisational strategies, the policies) and the unstated (what people actually do and how they behave). Aligned culture makes for a much more satisfying and rewarding place to work.

3. Individual Development

Going back to Herzberg's theory—three examples of motivators he named were "challenging work", "recognition" and "responsibility". We've talked about how one of the key aspects of your role as a leader is to develop the individuals within your team. This means providing work that challenges and ensuring that employees have responsibility and projects that grow and develop. It also means giving employees access to coaches and mentors who help to grow the individuals and provide regular feedback so that they know how they're doing. [29]

4. Reward and Recognition

Money isn't a motivator, but a perception of insufficient money is dissatisfying. Being clear with the team on how the remuneration structure works is key. Often issues with remuneration arise from a lack of transparency. Ask for clear explanations from HR or whoever set the structure in place and then share with your team how their salary is comprised, how the bonus system works, whether there's a link between performance and salary increases, how salary increases are calculated, whether there's a grading system and how that links to market value, CPI, etc.

If there are clear cases where a salary is out of sync with the grade, make sure you understand why that's the case and what (if anything) is being done to redress the situation. If you say you're going to take up a remuneration issue, take it up. Make sure you keep following it up until you receive an answer and share it—even if the answer isn't a positive one. Do all this. And then move on.

Reward and recognition isn't about salary or pay increases—that's good news, because often salary increases are hard to facilitate within an organisation, whereas reward and recognition can be easy and inexpensive.

A few important things to consider:

- A thank you goes a very long way. Even a handwritten card or a phone call for a job well done can be enormously powerful. When managing volunteers at the Melbourne 2006 Commonwealth Games, I found that out of all the reward and recognition schemes we had in place, the thing that they most appreciated was when Chairman Ron Walker came around and personally thanked each volunteer for their involvement.

- Reward and recognition fails when it's generic. This is all about the individual and what motivates them. For some, being recognised in a group by a senior leader may be very powerful; for others, they would rather crawl away and die than be called out in front of a group. For some, a thank you is all that's needed; for others, recognition such as flowers, dinner or a voucher is well received. The key here is to know what makes your team members tick. If you're recognising a team, then consider that for some people going bowling is torture and may not be considered a reward at all. Think about what makes the individual tick – one colleague commented that the best thank you and reward was some time off and that it had a disproportionate value in terms of being able to do things that you'd usually not be able to do during the day.

- Make it timely: it's no good recognising someone months after the event.

- Be appropriate: make sure the recognition or reward is consistent with the effort.

- Be consistent: if you're going to recognise and reward effort, then do it consistently.

- It doesn't have to be expensive, just thoughtful.

- A reward can be access to more challenging projects, an external coach or mentor, or some other personal development.

The story that has always stuck with me is from many years ago, when a facilitator was talking about the power of the appropriate "thank you". She described how she had been working for many, many months on a project. When it finally came to a successful conclusion, she came in the next morning to find a wrapped parcel on her desk. She had an affinity for a particular book that meant a great deal to her, and when she opened the parcel, she found a first edition copy of this book that her manager had found and bought for her as a thank you. In relative terms, this book was not that expensive compared with other "rewards" such as dinners out, weekends away, but its impact was so very powerful. Her manager had worked out what reward would truly be significant to her. And decades later, she is still talking about it.

TAKE A MOMENT

Do you know your organisational "why"? Think about your organisational values. Is there a disconnect between the stated values and what happens on a day-to-day basis? How could you work to change that?

Think about how you recognise and reward your team. Do you say thank you often enough?

STICKY MESSAGES :: A VERY SHORT RECAP

- Motivation isn't all about rah-rah speeches.
- Four elements are needed to motivate employees:
  1. Start with "why"
  2. Cultural alignment
  3. Individual development
  4. Reward and recognition
- Reward and recognition aren't necessarily about more money, but are always about the individual.
- The power of a thank you can be enormous.

RESOURCES

There are plenty of great resources on www.dowhatyousay.com.au including Simon Sinek's TED video "Start with Why".

Tool # 9: Delegate

Never tell people how to do things. Tell them what to do and they will surprise you with their ingenuity.

—General George Smith Patton Jr.

Oh how I love "Why I Can't Delegate" excuses. Of all the tools, delegation has the greatest amount of excuses for why it can't be done.

"I can't delegate the work" because:

- They don't know how to do it.
- They will make a mistake.
- It's quicker for me to do it.
- I don't trust them.
- I don't have time to show them how to do the work.
- It's my job.
- I like doing this work.
- I want to stay in touch.
- My boss expects me to do it.

And so on and so on.

As we've discussed, your job isn't necessarily to do the work—it's to get the work done. And often the way that you get the work done is by delegating it to your team. If you don't trust them, if they don't have the skills, if you don't have the time to do the work: that all reflects on you, rather than them. This is your job. If your team members don't have the right skills, it's up to you to give them those skills or move them out of the team. And yes, initially it will take more time. And yes, they will make mistakes—that's how people learn.

Go back to the definition of a leader. It is about growing and developing your people. It is about leading your team towards the organisational purpose. It is not necessarily about doing the work.

Comparing responsibility with accountability—what do they mean?

A quick aside here, often there is confusion between the words accountability and responsibility. This definition helps clarify this:

> *The main difference between responsibility and accountability is that responsibility can be shared while accountability cannot. Being accountable means being not only responsible for something but also ultimately answerable for your actions. When two people are accountable, no one is accountable.*[44]

You can ensure that people are given responsibility for undertaking the work, while still maintaining accountability for it.

We know that employees want challenging work that provides them with growth and development. Delegation is one key way for you to allow them that kind of work. This frees you up to do the work that you, as a leader, should be doing.

TAKE A MOMENT

What are your delegation excuses? What could you delegate from your list of responsibilities now? What's stopping you? What would you need to put in place to enable this? What would you need to put in place to be excited about delegating work?

STICKY MESSAGES :: A VERY SHORT RECAP

- Delegation is a key leadership skill.

- It reflects poorly on you rather than your team if you aren't able to delegate.

- Know the difference between accountability and responsibility.

RESOURCES

There are plenty of great resources on www.dowhatyousay.com.au that are worth a look.

Tool #10: Leading Through Change

*Change will not come if we wait for some other
person or some other time. We are the ones we've been
waiting for. We are the change that we seek.*

—Barack Obama

It's often said that the only constant is change. This is certainly true of leading in today's era: there's often no let-up from the onslaught of changes. This has led to a new level of complexity in leadership. It has also led to organisations that are full of change-weary employees. In such environments, inspiring, engaging and motivating can be hard.

Erica Fox and Nate Boaz have this to say in their article *Change Leader, Change Thyself:* "McKinsey research and client experience suggest that half of all efforts to transform organisational performance fail either because senior manager don't act as role models for the change, or because people defend the status quo. In other words, despite the stated change goals, people on the ground tend to behave as they did before".[45]

Research from Wayne Cascio backs this up, showing that "15 per cent of transformational projects are successful, while the rest fail miserably".[46]

Some Change Approaches You Can Use

A key component to the introduction of any change is the realisation that organisations don't change: the people within those organisations change. You need to reach each individual in a way that's meaningful for him or her. As with reward and recognition, what works for one employee may not work for another.

The Change Management experts, PROSCI® have a change model, ADKAR®, which says that any change effort needs the following:

- Awareness (What is the change about?)

- Desire (Do I want to change? How will it affect me?)

- Knowledge (Do I have the skills to make the change?)

- Ability (Do I have the ability and mindset to make the change?)

- Reinforcement (How is the change to be reinforced?)[47]

I like this model. It's simple and each step builds on the last to be self-sustaining.

You can also use the Switch Model, which uses the elephant and rider analogy. It's based on work by Jonathan Haidt in his book *The Happiness Hypothesis*[48], and followed up by Chip and Dan Heath in their book *Switch*.

The Heath brothers describe this analogy as follows:

> *Haidt says that our emotional side is an Elephant and our rationale side is its Rider. Perched atop the Elephant, the Rider holds the reins and seems to be the leader. But the Rider's control is precarious because the Rider is so small relative to the Elephant. Anytime the six-ton Elephant and the Rider disagree about which direction to go, the Rider is going to lose. He's completely overmatched.[49]*

Often, we think about change in terms of appealing to the rational side, without taking into account the emotional side, the Elephant that is so very, very powerful.

The Switch model asks:

- *Have you appealed to the intellectual/rational arguments?*
- *Have you appealed to the emotional?*
- *Have you cleared all the roadblocks and is the path "free" to make the change?[49]*

Some Tips for Managing Through Change

1. Send a Postcard

It's very hard for people to get their heads around what change means for them if they can't see its end point or visualise what it might look like or mean for them. Why is this change happening? What will it look like? Send a postcard of the future to your team so that there's something to inspire and engage them. If you can't paint the picture, then find out why.

2. Live the Change

It's equally hard for a team to change or become enthusiastic about a change if their leader is actively showing signs that they don't agree with or don't want to engage with it. "Do as I say, not as I do" has never proven to be more powerful than in change management. If you're saying one thing while doing another, you have very little chance of getting your team on board with the change. You also diminish your credibility. Take ownership of the change.

3. Communicate, Communicate, Communicate

Even if the message is that there's no news, that's still news. Keep talking. Keep communicating. Remember that people need to hear a message seven times before it sinks in. Think about what your team wants to know. What's changing? What's staying the same? How will it impact me? Why are we doing this? What's in it for me? Remember too that people want to hear strategy and long-term vision from the most senior leaders, but information about how the change will impact on them from their day-to-day leader.

4. Be Resilient

Change is hard. People get change-weary. Other changes get introduced over the top of the first change, diverting attention and resources. Priorities change, personnel change. One of the key elements of leading through change is to recognise change-weariness and build resilience in yourself and your team.

5. Embrace the Resistors

In every time of change there will be the naysayers, the resistors, the critics. The trick is to hear what they have to say. There will be useful messages in their resistance that you can use to build a stronger change effort. Perhaps you haven't sold the message clearly enough. Perhaps there's more work to be done on building awareness or desire. Or perhaps there's some roadblock removal that will deal with the resistance. Ignore resistors at your peril!

6. Don't make change for change's sake

As one colleague reflected, when a new leader comes along they generally want to make changes to stamp their mark and show that they are being proactive and 'deserve the new role'. Some make changes for the sake of the future of the company, some make changes for the sake of the team environment, some make changes to keep their big bosses/ board happy and some make changes for the sake of making changes that aren't necessarily effective or the right changes. Be aware of WHY you as a leader want to make changes and how it will affect each layer of the company and how you as a leader will address, communicate and deal with this.

TAKE A MOMENT

Think about all the change efforts that are currently in place within your team. Do you have resistors? What's their resistance? Is there any validity in what they're saying?

Can you somehow build this into your change effort?

Think about your own role within the change. How are you acting? Is it a case of do what I say, not what I do?

STICKY MESSAGES :: A VERY SHORT RECAP

- Leading through change is hard.

- Models such as ADKAR ®and Switch provide simple frameworks through which to think about change.

- What's the postcard for the future? Does it look enticing?

- Communicate, communicate, communicate, and then communicate some more.

- Embrace the resistors—they have a message for you that can be helpful.

- Think about WHY you are making the change (if it is you that it making it)

RESOURCES

There are plenty of great resources on www.dowhatyousay.com.au including some interesting research from McKinsey.

PART 3
Your Mindset

Choosing Your Mindset

If, like those with the growth mindset, you believe you can develop yourself, then you're open to accurate information about your current abilities, even if it's unflattering. What's more, if you're oriented toward learning, as they are, you need accurate information about your current abilities in order to learn effectively.

—Carol S. Dweck

Much of what we've discussed so far concerns thinking about how you do things and making some changes along the way. It's about growing and developing. It's about learning and trying new things: some that will work for you, some that may not. It's also about being a bit courageous along the way.

There are a few books I've mentioned that are absolute classics and must-reads. Another such book is *Mindset* by Carol S. Dweck. *Mindset* is the popularisation of many decades of research from Dr Dweck, who specialises in achievement and success. It's a fascinating book, partly due to the application of her work in leadership, coaching, schools, parenting and relationships, and partly due to the subject matter itself.

At the heart of Dr Dweck's theory is that there are two main types of individual:

> …those with a "fixed mindset" and those with a "growth mindset". The former group have a "fixed" good or bad view of their ability, whether it's their intellect, sporting or musical prowess. The latter believe that they always have the ability to develop and grow… [50]

Having a mindset that says you can always grow, develop and improve is absolutely critical to being a great leader, because being a great leader means being open to feedback, new ways of doing things and new ways of working.

Vulnerability and Failure

Of course the reason that many people aren't open to thinking with a growth mindset is that they are afraid—afraid mainly of failing, and afraid of being vulnerable.

But Brené Brown's *Daring Greatly*, discussed earlier, presents evidence that the reverse of those fears is true. According to Brown, being vulnerable actually improves your leadership rather than causing you to be a failure.[38] And as research in the *Experiencing Trustworthy Leadership report* shows, people are more likely to trust leaders when they are human, when they show vulnerabilities, when they admit their mistakes[28].

Peta Slocombe, a psychologist and leadership coach, has previously given me her perspective on this, when she wrote:

In addition to what the literature says, we see leaders every day—in counselling, coaching, workplace conflict consultancy and a range of other settings— where they are not at their best. It is clear to me that if you can't manage your own emotions, regulate your thoughts, and be vulnerable from time to time about your own developmental tasks, you will end up paying the price for it. We can't be "connected and authentic" in one area of our lives and ruthless and inauthentic in another. Stress, personal relationship breakdown, reduced work satisfaction and difficulty with relationships in general result. Good leadership means good relationships and the ability to keep adapting to change. To put it bluntly, inauthentic leadership is not sustainable.

This weekend I heard a panel of some of Australia's top sports coaches talking about the most sought-after athlete qualities. They mirror some of the best leadership advice of our time in agreeing that two things create success and high performance—personal authenticity on and off the field; and humility or openness to learning.

If that is high performance, and what we see of leaders engaging in poor behaviour or inauthentic leadership is high stress, conflict and personal turmoil, then the choice is clear. Good management is one thing. Good leaders, career-long, authentic leaders, are quite another ...[51]

Strengths and Weaknesses

As Marcus Buckingham and Donald O. Clifton state in Now Discover your Strengths, *"..the real tragedy of life is not that each of us don't have enough strengths, it's that we fail to use the ones we have"*.[52]

Or as Brian Cook says:

> *What unique skills or traits do I have that will give me leadership longevity and assist my organisation in gaining competitive advantage?*[1]

For many years, the trend was to look for your weaknesses, and then work on a plan to "fix" them. Indeed, many organisations still use this as their approach to development. However, for some time a new approach has been popular: look to your strengths and build on those. The idea being that it's easier to work on something that you're already good at than fix something you'll only ever be mediocre at. Marcus Buckingham (he of *First, Break All the Rules* fame) has beautifully illustrated this in his second book, *Now, Discover Your Strengths*. As Buckingham says:

> *The great organisation must not only accommodate the fact that each employee is different, it must capitalise on these differences. It must watch for clues to each employee's natural talents and then position or develop each employee so that his or her talents are transformed into bona fide strengths.*[52]

There is something unique about your strengths that, if nurtured, can allow your individual approach to leadership to be authentic and powerful and unique. Perhaps this is the way that you approach one on one conversations, perhaps it is about how you craft a message, perhaps it is about how you rally the troops when under pressure. Whatever your specific strengths are, knowing, understanding and exploiting them can be a very powerful approach to authentic and genuine leadership.

Note that building on your strengths is not the same as ignoring your weaknesses. There will always be aspects that need to be brought up to an appropriate standard. Rather, you have a much better chance at excelling in something that you already have an innate strength or talent in, than in something that you are only ever mediocre in at best. There is the often-quoted example of Tiger Woods, who has a very obvious weakness in his bunker play. He has been quite open in his approach that he worked on this area of his play sufficiently so that it was no longer a barrier to his success, and then returned to working on the areas of his play that he truly excelled in.[52]

To help you identify your specific strengths and talents, you could read *Now, Discover your Strengths* and take the online StrengthsFinder© Test.[53] You could also do a homemade version of this by sending out a SurveyMonkey® questionnaire to colleagues, bosses past and present, friends and family asking them to identify your strengths. You might be surprised by what comes back.

For Your Improvement, the book we talked about in Part One, is also a great resource for identifying how you can further capitalise on your strengths whilst also working on aspects of your leadership that may be career limiting.[18]

TAKE A MOMENT

Read *Now, Discover Your Strengths* and take the StrengthsFinder© Test to discover your strengths. Alternatively, ask 20 people to email you your strengths. What will you do with that information now? How can you build on this to create a leadership approach that suits you best?

STICKY MESSAGES :: A VERY SHORT RECAP

- *Mindset, Daring Greatly* and *Now, Discover Your Strengths* are three key books in identifying the core of getting to grips with your leadership.

  - Work on your weaknesses so that they're not derailers, then lead according to your strengths and your talents.

  - Be vulnerable, be prepared to fail, and be prepared to try new things and for some of them not to work.

  - Be open to growth, both for you and your team.

RESOURCES

There are plenty of great resources on www.dowhatyousay.com.au including a useful summary of why working on your strengths is so important.

Fears and Excuses
(Otherwise Known as the Lizard Brain)

Fear is the best compass you have that you are on the right track.

—*Seth Godin*

The good thing about all the tools this book has provided is that they'll give you the courage to lead better, building on your inherent strengths and the things that make you who you are. But there is something to watch out for—and that is our lizard brain.

Seth Godin explains the lizard brain in *Linchpin*, one of the key books I recommend you read after finishing this one. He talks about the daemon, which is the

> ... *source of great ideas, groundbreaking insights, generosity, love, connection and kindness.*

But also, importantly, resistance:

> *Your lizard brain, the part that the daemon has no control over, is working overtime to get you to shut up, sit down and do your (day) job. It will invent stories, illnesses, emergencies and distractions in order to keep the genius bottled up. The resistance is afraid.*

Godin goes on to explain how the very old reptile part of our brain is the amygdala, which is responsible for survival and other wild-animal traits:

> *This mini brain takes over whenever you are angry, afraid, aroused, hungry or in search of revenge. It's only recently that our brains evolved to allow big thoughts, generosity, speech, consciousness, and yes, art. When you look at a picture of the brain, the new part is what you see: the neocortex. That's the wrinkly part on the outside. It's big but it is weak. In the face of screaming resistance from the amygdala, the rest of your brain is helpless. It freezes and surrenders. The lizard takes over and tries to protect itself.[2]*

The lizard part of our brains is great in a "fight or flight" situation, but very unhelpful the rest of the time. It will rationalise against changes with any number of excuses. And these excuses will seem very sensible, very rationale, very believable. These excuses will stop you making the changes you want or need to.

Godin's explanation in *Linchpin* shows how we can rationalise away almost anything for fear of doing something different. As he says:

> *… the hard part is distinguishing between quitting because the resistance wants you to (bad idea) or because the resistance doesn't want you to (great idea). The goal is to quit the tasks you're doing because you're hiding on behalf of the lizard brain and to push through the very tasks the lizard fears.[2]*

Michelle Bridges has built a multimillion-dollar empire on helping people to get fit and healthy and lose weight. She knows all about the lizard brain, as one of the first exercises she gets her recruits to do—before they've even started on the programme— is to list excuses around the "why" they can't exercise or eat healthily. Getting the mind in the right place is so important to affecting any lasting change.

This exercise is a great one to do before considering any change you are trying to make, as it prompts a really rational look at the excuses we tell ourselves. There's another way to look at this, and that is—what's the payoff for staying the same? For example, the payoff for not losing weight is that you can continue to eat and drink whatever you feel like without regard for the consequences. Being clear on the stories we tell ourselves is a really good starting point for any change.

Underlying Assumptions

I asked Amanda Alldrick, an ontological coach, for her views on how underlying assumptions impact leadership effectiveness. She writes:

> *Leadership effectiveness is influenced by both competency and internal states of being. As leaders, our decisions and behaviours are underpinned by our internal assumptions and core belief systems that shape the way we respond to our world. Our internal assumptions and core beliefs act as a filter when deciphering information and making decisions. A great deal of evidence is emerging to suggest that effective leadership is influenced by both demonstrated*

leadership competencies and emotionally aware behaviours; that is, an awareness of our internal states of being.

As leaders it is critical to understand what the internal assumptions and core beliefs are that drive our behaviours. We seek to identify what it is that makes us tick, why we think the way we do. Our assumptions are what we believe to be true and sit below the stories that run in our minds, in our inner core. We filter information and make sense of the world through these stories.

So how does this impact leadership? We make decisions based on these filters, sometimes consciously and sometimes without realising. As human beings we default to our habits of thought, mostly without even knowing we are doing it. By bringing awareness to these habits of thought we start to develop a greater sense of our reactions and begin to take control of our responses.

In other words, we start to choose the way we behave and respond, rather than react[ing] through habit. A quick way to start bringing awareness to this is to consider an assumption that you hold. Once you have identified the assumption, check in to consider if this is an assumption that only you hold or if it is one generally held by most people. When we question this further, we start to develop a sense of our own core truth and what is meaningful for us. We can start to explore where this assumption comes from and how it is serving us. As leaders, this is critical to identify what filters we have in place that impact our effectiveness in leading others and achieving our goals. The crucial questions to ask are: What assumptions am I making here and how [are they] serving me? How [are they] serving others? Is there a more resourceful way to be?

The Impostor Syndrome

In amongst all this, be aware of the impostor syndrome. That little voice in your head that says: *I'm not good enough, I am a fraud. When will they discover that I don't really know what I'm talking about?* The impostor syndrome is well documented:

> *Impostor syndrome can be defined as a collection of feelings of inadequacy that persist even in [the] face of information that indicates that the opposite is true. It is experienced internally as chronic self-doubt and feelings of intellectual fraudulence. The impostor syndrome is associated with highly achieving, highly successful people.*[55]

It was originally associated with women, but recent research indicates that men suffer in similar numbers.[55]

Donny Walford, is the founder of Behind Closed Doors and Bottom Line, a leadership and networking academy for CEOs and board members. When I interviewed her for this book, she had this to say on the impostor syndrome:

> *They feel uncomfortable having older or more experienced people reporting to them, that they don't know it all and someone is going to tap them on the*

shoulder and say that they are a fraud. It's about confidence and time—time in the role. The team will learn to respect you, as you will them. Don't be afraid to admit you don't know it all and you rely on them and their knowledge. You have strengths and attributes they don't possess so you complement and leverage from each other. Play to your strengths and only fight the good fight. Don't take things personally and definitely don't overanalyse what is said ...

The impostor syndrome is a state of mind. Yes, men suffer from it too, but they "bluff" it better than women. They are better at "faking it until you make it". Do whatever improves your confidence because with improved confidence and self-belief you won't suffer from the impostor syndrome. You will feel comfortable in your own skin.[56]

TAKE A MOMENT

Think about a change you would like to make. Be aware of your reactions to those thoughts. What are you feeling? Is it fear? What is your head telling you about the change? Perhaps about why you "can't" do it, or about why it would be risky. Think about using the Michelle Bridges approach and take a long hard look at all the excuses you are using. What would it take for you to feel excited about the change you want to make rather than fearful (or any other negative emotion)?

STICKY MESSAGES :: A VERY SHORT RECAP

- The amygdala is very old and very strong and will provide resistance to any change. Be aware of this and the excuses your lizard brain comes up with. A great way of overcoming these excuses is to take a rational look at them.

- Fear isn't necessarily a bad thing—it can be a great compass, showing that you are on your way to some new, worthwhile change.

- We all have underlying assumptions. The trick is to understand the assumptions you're making and the impact they have on your behaviour.

- There are ways to overcome the imposter syndrome: play to your strengths, don't think you have to know it all, "fake it until you make it" and be open to learning, learning, learning all the time.

RESOURCES

There are plenty of great resources on www. dowhatyousay.com.au including a fabulous TED talk from Elizabeth Gilbert on the brain, which supplements what Seth Godin has to say.

Changing Perceptions

*A good leader shoulders the blame, but shares the
credit. Both talking and walking with staff engenders
loyalty and trust.*

—*Megan Quinn*

One question I'm often asked by emerging leaders is how to
change people's perceptions of them. This often comes up when
the leader has been working in the organisation for some time
and has recently been promoted. There may be commonly held
perceptions and views of that person's work style, some of which
may not be that flattering. Or, may not accurately reflect the way
that you want to be perceived going forward.

You're reading this book because you want to be the best leader
that you can be. This may mean taking a hard look at internal—
and perhaps external—perceptions of you and thinking about
what you may want to change.

Tips to Change Perceptions

1. Is It True, or Is It Your Self-Talk?

Go back to the "impostor syndrome" we talked about in the
"Fears and Excuses" section. I'm not talking about your own

self-talk: I'm talking about what your peers, colleagues, team members, bosses and customers would say about you and your leadership style.

2. Seek Accurate Feedback and Data Before Acting

If you suspect that the feedback won't be positive, check it out before acting. Act on facts rather than fiction. One person I coached was absolutely certain that his team would describe him in a particular (very negative) way. He was reacting and responding based on this assumption. So we did a quick survey to find out the truth—and he couldn't have been more wrong. Yes, there were things he could have done differently or improved on, but by and large the perceptions of him by his team were very positive.

3. So It's True

If you have accurate data that perceptions of you need to be changed, take a good look at what it is that people are saying. Is it true? Is it fair? Could they be right? You may need help with this—either with a trusted internal colleague, someone in HR or a coach. Work out what you want to change. Be specific. Think about the particular behaviours and actions that fall into the category, rather than just a general overarching statement. Think about what it would look like if you were to demonstrate new behaviours and actions.

4. Build Trust

Leadership is about getting results in a way that builds and inspires trust rather than erodes it. It means that the manner in which you do things is as important as the end result. It also means that you are more likely to get things done next time, if you act in a way that builds and establishes trust. Doing things the rough and ready way can achieve the end result, but at a cost that reduces or destroys trust. I like to think of it as a bank account. When you act in a way that builds trust, there are steady deposits that accrue interest over time. When you act in a way that destroys trust, this can mean a significant withdrawal of the account, leaving you in a deficit and having to pay interest rather than earn it.[58]

In changing perceptions, you need to build trust that has otherwise been eroded. Stephen M.R. Covey's *The Speed of Trust* is a great book that shows how to build trust and rebuild step by step. This can help you in so many ways, not only in changing perceptions.

Key to this is the point that Covey makes that it is not just the behaviours or actions themselves that contribute to trust (or lack of trust), but critically, how those behaviours are perceived by others[59]. Dr Adam Fraser, author of *The Third Space* goes further and explains that we excuse and minimize our own behaviour due to circumstances but don't tolerate that very same behaviour in others.[62]

What I particularly love about Covey's work is that it gives practical tips around how to build trust. Whilst he does make the valid point that you can't control other people's responses to your efforts, his case for building and rebuilding a trust account is so compelling that it is worth it in almost any case.

5. Manage the Perceptions

It may be that the perceptions need managing rather than changing. Think about how you can do this. Is it something that you need a sponsor within the organisation to help you with? Do you need to plan by working with a coach or HR to show that the perceptions are inaccurate or unreasonable? If you don't have HR in your organisation, then who else can you use to help?

And lastly ...

6. Just Do It: Actions Speak Louder than Words

Another book from Seth Godin, *Poke the Box*, has this story:

> *Annie Downs works at the Mocha Club, a non-profit based in Nashville that raises money for the developing world by working with touring musicians. Last year she called her boss and said something she had never said before: "I've got an idea, and I'm going to start working on it tomorrow. It won't take a lot of time and it won't cost a lot of money, and I think it is going to work."*
>
> *With those two sentences, Annie changed her life. And she changed her organisation and the people it serves. You're probably wondering what her idea was. You may even be curious about how she pulled it off. That is the wrong question. The change was in her posture. The change was that for the first time in this job, Annie wasn't waiting for instructions, working through a to-do list, or reacting to incoming tasks. She wasn't*

handed initiative, she took it. Annie crossed a bridge that day. She became someone who starts something, someone who initiates, someone who is prepared to fail along the way if it helps her make a difference.[60]

When we want to change perceptions of ourselves, we can spend a lot of time pondering or blaming—or we can just get on and do it. Make a plan and carry it out. Start now. Try new things. Yes, you'll probably make more mistakes along the way. Yes, you'll misjudge some situations. Yes, it may be three steps forward, one step back. But remember this: if you keep doing what you always do, you'll keep getting what you always get.

Leading by walking around

There's another tip that is very handy in changing perceptions. Often employees build perceptions of their leaders based on inaccuracies, because they are never to be seen (think back to the ivory tower).

Taking a few minutes every day to walk (and critically) talk to your employees can do more to build positive perceptions than many other tools. Getting to know your employees names, a bit of their family circumstances, what football team they follow; it all adds up, it all adds a bit to the trust deposit account.

Being aware that you are always being watched, and that your actions speak louder than words is also critical. If you are trying to implement a safety culture, but don't follow your own safety guidelines to wear high visibility jackets, then don't expect your message to be taken very seriously.

TAKE A MOMENT

Is there an internal or external perception that you'd like to change about yourself? What is that? What's holding you back from addressing it? What would it take for you to feel comfortable about making the change? If you're not visible to your team and your employees, ask yourself why? What's holding you back?

Read *The Speed of Trust* and implement Godin's techniques.

Make a plan, and do it.

STICKY MESSAGES :: A VERY SHORT RECAP

- Perceptions can be changed—but before you do anything, make sure that your understanding of the perceptions is accurate and that it's not just your self-talk.

- If your understanding is accurate, make a plan, build trust, and use your sponsors.

- Most importantly, just do it!

- Leading by walking around is a key leadership tool.

RESOURCES

There are plenty of great resources on www.dowhatyousay.com.au including the Business Case for Trust from the Victorian Leadership Development Centre.

Creating Your Leadership Persona

It is never too late to be what you might have been.

- George Eliot

In the last chapter, we spent some time talking about changing perceptions and how you can go about doing this. So, it is a good time to also introduce the concept of a leadership persona, as it is a great illustration of how you can decide to change elements about your behaviours and create a new way of working, a new way of being, a new way of being perceived. This can be helpful if you are looking to change perceptions, but also where it is a fresh start in an organisation.

By this stage of the book, if you've been doing the **Take a Moment** exercises and referring to the other resources, you'll be starting to have a good idea of your leadership style, what your strengths are, and how you want to lead. Bear all that in mind as you keep reading.

So how do you go about creating your leadership persona? I asked leadership expert Justin Miles, Managing Partner, Melbourne of Generator Talent Group to explain. He writes:

Designing your Leadership Persona

It's a word that you don't see much in common use these days. "Persona" evolved from an ancient Greek term to describe the masks actors used in plays. Short of talent, an actor would put on a new mask or persona and play a different character within the same play.

This was first introduced to me by a consultant who taught a group of us presentation skills, drawing on an incredibly deep well of his experience from vaudeville theatre to coaching USA Presidential nominees for TV debates. The idea was that if you started practicing (or acting) with a different persona, you'd eventually become that person—you'd habituate these new behaviours into a new character, and that persona would become yours, and eventually you. It was a simple and effective way of working through a complex behavioural change.

I've drawn on this concept of the persona in a number of leadership programs, and know it's helped a range of leaders start to shift their effectiveness and impact on people. The persona construct helps people frame their thinking to be a leader first, and a functional expert second.

It starts by understanding that throughout your life, based on the way you view yourself and the world around you, you've formed an individual style and approach.

This is how you display your often-unconscious intentions to yourself and others, and how you express your role as a leader. Some of us have done this with more deliberation; others have just let it evolve.

Now, if you sought to consciously change elements of your leadership style, you might start to design a new persona. You might start to make deliberate choices relative to the elements you believe your role calls for what you should be thinking, doing, looking like, sounding like and acting like; where you should be making an impact; who you should influence; what risks you'll take and what you're striving to do and create.

Once you affirm the elements you've chosen are valid, you should seek to practice and employ them over time—that is, start to "wear" your new persona. As you wear the new persona more often, the elements are recorded indelibly in your subconscious mind and displayed habitually and become automatic.

Your persona becomes the new normal, the new you.

Here's how we explain the respective components:

1. The Role You Define

Leaders take personal accountability for specific things. With a clear sense of purpose and accountability they make it clear what they are here to do. The first step in designing your leadership persona is to ask yourself what kind of leader you are and what leadership means for you.

Considering these questions will shape your answers: What kind of leadership does the culture of my organisation demand? And, what kind of leadership does my team require of me? And, if you're willing to define your role as having accountability for things and people that you don't control ... magic will happen.

☕ TAKE A MOMENT ···

For each team you are a leader of, or a member of, finish this sentence: My role on this team is to ...

2. The Stand You Take

People are motivated to maintain the integrity of the self, and an outwardly stated commitment becomes the moment of truth for a leader. Great leaders take a position, and are willing to articulate it (state it out loud). The language you use is important—language conveys not only information but also commitment, and people act by stating commitments. Stating your commitment out loud is a bold promise. You need to place yourself in the future. Your stand should represent clear outcome-based goals.

TAKE A MOMENT

What is your core purpose; your statement of commitment? Have you clearly defined the performance ethic of your team and the teams you are on?

3. The Standard You Accept

The success of a business is a direct reflection of the strengths and weaknesses of its leaders. Individuals (and businesses) achieve the success that equates to their level of satisfaction and where you choose to be satisfied will determine the level of your success. For a lot of people, it's not what they know that leads to their success—it's more a result of what standard they are prepared to accept. That is why average is the enemy of great. Where you choose to be satisfied will ultimately determine the level of your success.

TAKE A MOMENT

How have you described the difference between "average performance" and "acceptable performance" for your team and your organisation? How long do you settle for average performance?

4. The Focus of Your Delivery

All we have is our time. The way we spend our time is our priorities, is our strategy. Your calendar knows what you really care about. Do you? How much of your time should you spend on real leadership issues? How much of your time do you spend on real leadership issues? You are your calendar—and calendars never lie. Leaders direct their energy towards what really matters. Your calendar knows what your focus is.

TAKE A MOMENT

Have a look at your calendar for the month just passed and the month ahead. What are the two processes you are spending most of your time on? What are the two processes you should be spending most of your time on?

5. The Impact You Make

How will the business measure your contribution? The essence of leadership is to define the outcomes required and align resources to deliver those outcomes. Delivering outcomes is what you're paid to do— effort is good, trying hard is to be applauded, missing occasionally is part of life. But ultimately, you have to make an impact and get things done, and cause situations to change for the better. Your business will measure your outcomes based on the things they can see or measure.

TAKE A MOMENT

What difference are you making in your organisation? What will people say about your legacy? What commitments to people have you got in play at the moment?

What's great about this concept of a leadership persona is that you can choose to change it. As with everything we have talked about so far in the book, you can choose to behave in a different way. You can consciously choose to act in a way that produces different results. The next part of this book shows you how you can be aware of your own and other's perceptions of you and how you can (if necessary) change those perceptions. Keep the concepts of the leadership persona in mind when you're thinking about changing perceptions or rebuilding trust.

STICKY MESSAGES :: A VERY SHORT RECAP

There are five elements to designing your leadership persona:

- The Role You Define
- The Stand You Take
- The Standard You Accept
- The Focus of Your Delivery
- The Impact You Make.

A leadership persona is an iterative process and it takes time to refine it. But, you can start to put on the mask, start acting differently, and start creating your new persona right now.

As you grow into and live your persona, people will notice, and then over time it won't feel like a mask anymore; it will be you.

RESOURCES

There are plenty of great resources on www.dowhatyousay.com.au that are worth a look.

PART 4

Looking Out for You

Helping Yourself to Grow (with the Help of a Mentor)

Take risks, develop networks and relationships with key influencers, identify mentors—both male and female—and get an internal and external sponsor to promote you to others.

—Donny Walford

Donny Walford knows a thing or two about leaders and leadership, and I think that her advice above is succinct and insightful.

Get a Mentor

Interestingly, in my interviews for this book, having access to a mentor has cropped up over and over again. So what is mentoring? This word so often gets confused with coaching and other developmental roles. But mentoring is quite specific.

Mentoring is most often defined as a professional relationship in which an experienced person (the mentor) assists another (the mentoree or mentee) in developing specific skills and knowledge that will enhance their professional and personal growth.

Brian Cook says:

> *Mentoring can be marvellous and it can be unimpressive. It is so important to find, even if you have to remunerate a mentor or mentors.[1]*

In our interview, Holly Ransom, the Young West Australian of the Year 2012, had this to say on mentoring:

> *I think it's critical that emerging leaders look for different avenues in which to improve their skills and their understandings of the workplace, and ultimately to get advice and guidance as how to best chart their career. Having mentors is a great way to do that, and for me they have been the single biggest contributor to my growth and development as a leader and as a person.[57]*

Here, Donny Walford answers my questions about mentoring:

How important do you think mentors are in leadership?

> *Very important: it's lonely at the top for both men and women, so a mentor becomes an important "support" for you in leadership positions and they will help you understand yourself and others better. Mentors improve you professionally as well as personally. The mentor is a very useful sounding board for testing new ideas and covering [of] various issues that arise in your professional and personal life.*

How would you recommend an emerging leader choose a mentor?

Understand what outcomes you want from the mentoring relationship. Ask people you trust whom they recommend could help you achieve your outcomes or identify a mentor from people you have met or heard of. They do not have to be in your industry sector. Make a personal approach. There are organisations that offer coaching and mentoring services and are adept at identifying a mentor for you. It's critical you meet with your proposed mentor to decide if you can work together before formalising the relationship.

What characteristics should they look for?

The most important aspect is trust—you must feel you can be open and honest with your mentor and that all discussions are confidential. They must be a good listener and ask good challenging and thought-provoking questions.

How can they tell that the relationship is working?

At the first meeting, Mentor and Mentee need to:
- *discuss expectations of the mentoring process and anticipated outcomes, and general objectives*
- *talk about ambitions, development goals, mutual expectations*
- *decide when and where to meet and for how long*
- *choose a time and place for mentoring sessions—if possible, away from your workplace.*

The mentee will know the relationship is working because they are being challenged and growing professionally and personally, and they are achieving their outcomes. If you are totally honest and open with your mentor and growing in confidence then the relationship is adding value.

Have you personally had a mentor who has helped you grow and develop as a leader?

I have had a series of informal mentors during my career and business life. As [I was] one of few women in senior management and executive roles there were few role models, so most of my mentors and role models have been men. My female role model is Carolyn Hewson AO. Carolyn only needs to make one suggestion or statement, or ask one thought-provoking question and you can go forward for another year based on that wisdom.[56]

TAKE A MOMENT

Think about Donny Walford's advice. What risks can you take to grow and develop your leadership? (Beware the lizard brain trying to stop you.) What networks are you already tapped into? Which ones can you tap into? Do you have a mentor? If not, who would you approach? Make a plan to do so.

STICKY MESSAGES :: A VERY SHORT RECAP

- Mentoring is not the same as coaching.
- Mentoring is a life-long process that may involve several or many mentors, or just one.

RESOURCES

There are plenty of great resources on www.dowhatyousay.com.au including the Lush TV interview between James Lush and Holly Ransom and Holly's podcasts on mentoring.

Looking Out for You

Do not set yourself up for failure by striving for work–life balance. Strive for work–life FLOW. Do what you love and love what you do.

—Donny Walford

There's a reason the airlines ask you to put your oxygen mask on before helping others—and it applies equally to leadership. You are no good to others if you're not fit and healthy yourself. You need to look after yourself first and foremost.

Being a leader of any sort in today's world is hard work. Almost every leader I spoke to for this book talked about how they looked after themselves first—how they prioritised exercise and fitness as a way not only to keep healthy, but also to manage stress and gain perspective. Donny Walford again:

> *Life and work … flows in with each other. Learn to be selfish—it's not a bad word. Learn to put some time away each week for you—to read a book, do exercise, lunch or coffee with a friend, go for a massage. Whatever your passion and enjoyment is—do it![56]*

This is all stuff we should already know: exercise, keep fit and healthy, minimise alcohol and other drugs, minimise caffeine, eat mostly healthy foods, have healthy relationships that enhance rather than detract from your life.

Managing Stress

This is one of the biggest issues that I talk through with the people I coach. Below are a few techniques I suggest to help them manage the stress of leading in today's world. The message here is that if these techniques aren't working, get help before the issue becomes too big.

1. Do Something (Rather than Just Worrying)

Ask yourself (in the cold light of day, away from the heat of the emotion): Is there anything specific I can do now that will move this forward? Is there a phone call I can make? Is there some specific action I can do or make happen that will change this situation? If yes, consider whether it really will move the situation forward. If so, do it.

2. Let It Go

If not, let it go. Really, at the end of the day, many things (and people) don't make sense—and won't make sense no matter how much analysis and time is spent on them. The answer that all parents perfect, "Just because," is sometimes the best one. Sometimes it is what it is, and you don't need to like it, but you do need to accept that there may not be anything you can do to change it. Often as soon as you genuinely and completely let go of the angst around something, it resolves itself on its own. Life can be funny like that.

3. The Shoebox Concept

Imagine you have shoeboxes in your closet and that difficult ideas, people and situations each have their own shoebox. You park the situation in the shoebox, put the lid on it, and put it back on the shelf until you're ready and able to re-examine it. Then you can bring it down, open it up and ask yourself the two questions above. It's so simple, but a great way of making sure that complex aspects of your life and work don't take up more airspace, thought or emotion than they need.[61]

4. Get Help

If none of the techniques above are working as a way to manage your stress, and it's getting out of control, get help. Seek advice from your HR department. Ask for a coach (internal or external). See if you have an Employee Assistance Programme either for counselling or access to stress management programmes—EAPs are almost always free to employees and their families, and can be a great source of external advice and support. Your GP can also be a good source of assistance on techniques to manage stress.

Managing Your Workload

Time and time again throughout this book we've talked about the role of a leader. Go back to the definitions at the beginning and also look at the tool on delegation. Emerging leaders are almost always doing too much because they're doing the wrong things. Make sure your team is doing their job and that you're doing yours. Remember that no one likes a martyr, and they're not terribly effective leaders either.

Go back to the changing perceptions section: do you need to sit with your boss and come to an agreement on your role and priorities, and how the workload fits into this? Do you need some help from an internal sponsor? Is there work that doesn't need to be done, either by you or at all? Be clever about how you spend your time.

On occasion, managing your workload is less about what you do and more about how you do it. If you suspect this might be you, again, seek help. There are some great productivity and time-management techniques and programmes that can really help you become more efficient and effective.

One person I coached came to the realisation that it was about managing his to-do list, rather than letting the to-do list manage him. He realised that trying to tick off every item every day meant that he was constantly rushing, constantly stressed and making mistakes. He changed his approach to view his list as a weekly guide rather than a daily dictate. He also put in place rules for himself: instead of going over pieces of work time and time again, he would complete the work in a measured way, then put it aside with a period diarised in the next 24 to 48 hours to review.

The result: he's completing more things on his to-do list, they are of better quality with more robust critical thinking, and he has time each day to do his reading, research and thinking, things he was never able to do in the past because he was always "so busy". He isn't working any additional hours (in fact, he's working less), but every indicator has improved.

He succeeded because he took a good look at what he was doing, asked himself whether he had to be doing it personally (was there a good opportunity for development in a team member?) and most importantly, how he was working. He also looked at aspects of work that he wanted to do but didn't have time for. He changed his approach and was disciplined about making the new approach work. And he used the coaching process to keep himself accountable for continuing the change.

Have a life

Perhaps one of the most effective ways to keep work in perspective is to ensure that work is not the only thing in your life. Having other aspects in your life that provide enjoyment is not only a great way to manage stress and provide relaxation, but also provides some attempt at the mystical work/life balance.

The catch 22 to this is that setting up and maintaining external interests can take time, which might feel like a commodity you don't have much of. But the benefits are well established and it is worth the effort and the persistence.

Zone out

There's an interesting trend happening around meditative mindfulness as a way to manage stress. This can be as simple as the myriad of apps that are available for use on your smartphone. These will take you through a combination of meditation/ breathing and mindfulness, often in just a few minutes a day. Or there's the current trend of colouring in for adults (stay with me on this), where you buy or download one of the many beautiful books or templates and spend a few minutes a day quietly colouring and contemplating. There is research on the benefits of this from a managing stress perspective, changing behaviour and enhancing creativity.[54]

TAKE A MOMENT

Do a quick stocktake of what Donny Walford calls your work–life flow. Is there anything you can do that would put you on a healthier path? If so, can you implement a plan to get on this path?

Think about your biggest stressors and apply the techniques above. Can you categorise them? Is there anything you can do, or do you need external help?

STICKY MESSAGES :: A VERY SHORT RECAP

- Look after yourself. Yes, that means eat well, drink less alcohol, exercise regularly and manage your stress.

- Think about other interests that may help with "balance".

- Actively manage your stress, don't just let it pile up.

- If your attempts to manage your stress aren't working, then get help. Use your Employee Assistance Programme or any other resources that the organisation provides.

RESOURCES

There are plenty of great resources on www.dowhatyousay.com.au including links to Johanna Basford's beautiful colouring in that you can download.

Your Legacy

*As times change ever more rapidly, it is ever easier
for us to fulfil Andy Warhol's prediction that we will
all be famous for fifteen minutes. But it is ever more
difficult to be remembered for fifteen years.*

Max Landsberg

There's an oft-quoted technique of thinking about yourself at your funeral (cheery, I know!), looking and listening to what people have to say about you. Often this technique is used to help people prioritise what's important in life before it's too late, but I think it can also be one of the most effective leadership tools around.

If you've read this far, then you have learnt many useful techniques that will help you build on your strengths and become a better leader. And of course, there are many more that I could have included. Implementing any one of them alone will improve your leadership skills. Of course, implementing them in concert will magnify the effects.

But perhaps the singularly most powerful tool that you can implement is the following version of the funeral technique.

What would you want people to be saying about you on hearing of your resignation? How will your team, peers, colleagues and customers be talking about you in years to come? What language will they use? Will they talk about you with affection or with anger? What anecdotes will they quote to sum you up?

So, what do you want your legacy to be? Write it down and be specific. Here are some ideas on what you can use to help you get there:

- Ask your HR department about getting 360-degree feedback.

- Get a coach and/or a mentor.

- Implement the techniques in this book.

- Think about your leadership persona

- Read, read, read, read.

- Seek feedback from your colleagues, your peers, your boss, your team, your customers, and your stakeholders.

- Ask yourself what you should start, stop and continue doing.

Now, what are *you* going to do to make this happen? Start now, start today. Find your courage to lead.

RESOURCES

There are plenty of great resources on www.dowhatyousay.com.au. Make sure you check them out – there's plenty there to continue the journey.

A final (and most important) note

I couldn't have contemplated writing this book without the enormous support and love that I receive every day from my family. To Alex, who doesn't ever blink an eyelid at my latest hair brained idea or scheme and is only supportive and constructive; to my Mum for her ongoing support, love and very helpful practical advice; and to my two little mischiefs who spent many an hour wondering why Mum was locked away buried under piles of books and papers—thank you and I love you all. Writing a book is not for the faint hearted, as it turns out, so thank you too to my friends and family for the constant encouragement to keep on going.

This book would not exist without the wisdom of the many that contributed to it. To those that I interviewed for the book: Brian Cook, Sonja Cox, Maggie Dent, Dr Penny Flett, Holly Ransom, Donny Walford and Dr Fiona Wood, my sincere thanks for your generosity of time and words and wisdom.

To those that have contributed with their expertise and words, my thanks to Jon Allen, Dr Margot Wood, Justin Miles, Rob Whitechurch, David Koutsoukis, Peta Slocombe, Jaine Edge and Amanda Alldrick. The book is better for your contribution to it.

To my early readers and those that gave valuable feedback. The book is all the better for your insights and feedback. Thank you to Martin Wandmaker, Dr Brendan Shaw, Vari Flay and Paula Flynn.

To those that I have coached, who gave me the inspiration for writing this book in the first place, thank you. Coaching is always as much about learning as it is about teaching.

To all those who brought my manuscript to life: Kate Goldsworthy for her editing, Cheryl Pech for proofing, editing and sense checking, Kristy Haines at Aviary Design for the website, Reece Spykerman for the beautiful cover, Kelly Exeter for the interior design and to Janelle Batstone for the images, thank you.

And finally to the wonderful Bernadette Jiwa. It wouldn't have happened without you. Thank you!

General References

1. Interview between Brian Cook and Tammy Tansley via email

2. Godin, S 2014, *Linchpin*. Hachette Digital, Jouve, France. Available from amazon.com [23 April 2015]

3. Interview with Maggie Dent and Tammy Tansley via email

4. Teitelbaum, D, 2014, *'Seth Godin is an ideas man'* Dumbo Feather, Edition 40, Third Quarter, p28

5. *Why Good Leaders make you feel safe,* 2014 (video file) Available from: http://www.ted.com/talks/simon_sinek_why_good_leaders_make_you_feel_safe [29 March 2015]

6. Church, M 2013, *Amplifiers*, Wiley, Queensland

7. Sutton, R 2007, HBR.org. March 17 2007. *Why I wrote the no asshole rule*, Available from: http://blogs.hbr.org/2007/03/why-i-wrote-the-no-asshole-rule/ [29 March 2015]

8. Schwartz, T, 2012, The Energy Project. July 11 2012. *Emotional Contagion Can Take Down Your Whole Team*, Available from: http://theenergyproject.com/blog/emotional-contagion-can-take-down-your-whole-team [29 March 2015]

9. Lombardo, M & Eichinger, R 2006, *The Leadership Machine,* Lominger Limited

10. McKellin Institute, 2012, *McKellin Productivity Report,* Available from: http://mckellinstitute.org.au/wp-content/uploads/2012/11/McKell_Productivity_Report_A4.pdf [29 March 2015]

11. Davenport, T & Harding S, 2010, *Manager Redefined: the Competitive Advantage.* Jossey Bass Books. San Francisco, CA Available from: amazon.com [29 March 2015]

12. Gallup.com 2013. *State of the Global Workforce 2013,* Available from: http://ihrim.org/Pubonline/Wire/Dec13/GlobalWorkplaceReport_2013.pdf [1 April 2015]

13. iHR Australia, 2014. *Six figure payout for bullied grandmother,* Available from: http://ihraustralia.com/hr-workplace-relations-news/six-figure-payout-for-bullied-grandmother [29 March 2015]

14. Huffington Post, 2014. *Market Basket Drama Ends.* Available from: http://www.huffingtonpost.com/2014/08/27/market-basket-drama_n_5726776.html [29 March 2015]

15. Biro, M, forbes.com, 2014 *How to be a good leader, get real,* Available from: http://www.forbes.com/sites/meghanbiro/2014/08/29/how-to-be-a-good-leader-get-real/ [29 March 2015]

16. Frankel, L, *Preventing Individual's Career Derailment,* Available from: http://www.drloisfrankel.com/resources/free_articles.html [29 March 2015]

17. Zenger J, & Folkman, J, HBR.org, *The Skills Leaders Need at Every Level,* July 30 2014. Available from https://hbr.org/2014/07/the-skills-leaders-need-at-every-level/ [30 March 2015]

18. Lombardo M & Eichinger R, 2009 *FYI: For Your Improvement,* Lominger Limited.

19. Kotter, J, *Management is still not leadership,* January 2013. HBR.org/blog. Available from http://blogs.hbr.org/2013/01/management-is-still-not-leadership/ [29 March 2015]

20. Collin, R, insidehr.com.au *2013 Leadership and Management: Same or Different*, Available from: http://www.insidehr.com.au/leadership-and-management-same-or-different/ [29 March 2015]

21. Definition from dictionary.com [Online] [29 March 2015]

22. Mindtools.com, 2015, *Leadership Styles*, Available from: http://www.mindtools.com/community/pages/article/newLDR_84.php?route=pages/article/newLDR_84.php [30 March 2015]

23. Mindtools.com, 2015. *Leadership Styles*, Available from: http://www.mindtools.com/community/pages/article/newLDR_84.php?route=pages/article/newLDR_84.php [30 March 2015]

24. Bennis, W & Thomas, R, HBR.org, 2002, *Crucibles of Leadership*, September 2002. HBR.org. Available from: https://hbr.org/2002/09/crucibles-of-leadership [29 March 2015]

25. Tansley, T, tammytansley.com.au, 2013, *Crucibles of Leadership*, June 18 2013. Available from http://www. tammytansley.com.au/blog/the-crucibles-of-leadership. html#.VKT0kMYz4hk [30 March 2015]

26. Tansley, T, tammytansley.com.au, 2013, *Telstra Business Woman of the Year Sonja Cox,* June 23 2014. Available from http://www.tammytansley.com.au/ blog/2013-telstra-wa-business-woman-of-the-year-sonja-cox.html#.VKT1ZMYz4hk [29 March 2015]

27. Locke, J, talentculture.com, 2014, *The Dark Side of Leadership*, June 16 2014. Available from http://www. talentculture.com/leadership/power-the-dark-side-of-leadership [29 March 2015]

28. Hope Hailey V & Gustafsson, S. 2014, *Experiencing trustworthy leadership*. Research Report. London: CIPD.

29. Mindtools.com, 2015. *Herzberg's Motivators and Hygiene Factors*, Available from: http://www.mindtools.com/ community/pages/article/herzberg-motivators-hygiene-factors.php?route=pages/article/newTMM_74.php [30 March 2015]

30. Interview with Dr Penny Flett and Tammy Tansley in person

31. Creasy T & Hiatt J (eds) 2009, *Best Practices in Change Management,* 2009 edition, PROSCI Research, USA

32. Tansley, T, hcamag.com, 2013, *Combatting Negative Bias in Communication*, 2 April 2013. Available from http://www.hcamag.com/opinion/combating-negative-bias-in-communication-174057.aspx [29 March 2015]

33. PROSCI, *5 Tips For: Better Communications,* Available from: http://www.change-management.com/tutorial-5-tips-communication.htm [30 March 2015]

34. Interview with Dr Fiona Wood and Tammy Tansley via email

35. Lencioni, P, 2002, *The Five Dysfunctions of a Team*, Jossey Bass, San Francisco

36. Mindtools, 2015, *Forming, Storming, Norming and Performing,* Available from: http://www.mindtools.com/community/pages/article/newLDR_86.php [29 March 2015]

37. Help Me HR. 2014. *Five Tips to Effective Workplace Conversations,* December 5 2014. Available from: http://helpmehr.com.au/five-tips-to-effective-workplace-conversations/ [29 March 2015]

38. Brown, B, 2012, *Daring Greatly,* Penguin Group (USA) Inc, New York

39. Lush Digital, Justin Langer, (Video file) Available from: http://lushdigital.com/ltv/justin/ [29 March 2015]

40. Landsberg, M 1996, *The Tao of Coaching*, Profile Books, London

41. *How Lululemon's CEO learned to lead*, 2011, (Video file) Available from: http://money.cnn.com/video/news/2011/10/28/best_advice_christina_day.cnnmoney/ [30 March 2015]

42. Martin Luther King, I have a Dream speech, 2013. (Video File) Available from: https://www.youtube.com/watch?v=3vDWWy4CMhE [29 March 2015]

43. *Start with Why* – Simon Sinek TED Talk, 2013 (Video File) Available from: https://www.youtube.com/watch?v=sioZd3AxmnE [29 March 2015]

44. Diffen.com *Accountability vs Responsibility*. Available from: http://www.diffen.com/difference/Accountability_vs_Responsibility [30 March 2015]

45. Boaz N & Fox E, McKinsey.com, 2014, *Change Leader, Change Thyself*. March 2014, Available from: http://www.mckinsey.com/insights/leading_in_the_21st_century/change_leader_change_thyself [30 March 2015]

46. HR Daily, 2014. *Don't let leadership failures derail business transformations*. Available at http://www.hrdaily.com.au/nl06_news_selected.php?act=2&nav=1&selkey=3190 [29 March 2015]

47. Hiatt J & Creasey T, 2003, *CHANGE Management*, Prosci Research, Colorado, USA

48. Haidt J, 2006, *The Happiness Hypothesis*, Basic Books, New York

49. Heath C & Heath D, 2010, *Switch*, Broadway Books, New York

50. Dweck C, 2012, *Mindset: How You Can Fulfil Your Potential, Constable and Robinson*, UK. Available from amazon.com [30 March 2015]

51. Tansley, T, tammytansley.com.au (2012) *101 Series: Great Leadership,* November 25 2012. Available from: <http://www.tammytansley.com.au/blog/101-series-great-leadership.html#.VKT0XsYz4hk> [29 March 2015]

52. Buckingham M, & Clifton O, 2001 *Now, Discover your Strengths,* Gallup.com. Available from amazon.com [30 March 2015]

53. Clifton Strengths Finder. 2015. Available from: www.strengthsfinder.com [30 March 2015]

54. Keating, E, smartcompany.com.au, *2015 Businesses Turn to Colouring Books*, 9 April 2015, Available from: http://www.smartcompany.com.au/leadership/46363-businesses-turn-to-colouring-books-for-employees-are-they-the-key-to-a-stress-free-workplace.html# [17 April 2015]

55. Tansley, T, behindcloseddoors.com, 2014, *It is Lonely at the Top*, 19 June 2014. Available from: http://behindcloseddoors.com/it-is-lonely-at-the-top-but-it-doesnt-have-to-be/ [30 March 2015]

56. Interview with Donny Walford and Tammy Tansley via email

57. Tansley, T, tammytansley.com.au 2014, *Holly Ransom: It's more important to be interested than interesting,* 30 June 2014. Available from: http://www.tammytansley.com.au/blog/holly-ransom-its-more-important-to-be-interested-than-interesting.html#.VKT0DsYz4hk [30 March 2015]

58. Baines, G & Covey S & Merrill, R *The Topline Summary of Speed of Trust 2014*, BB Publishing. Available via amazon.com [30 March 2015]

59. Covey, S, 2002, *Speed of Trust*, Free Press, New York

60. Godin, S, 2011, *Poke that Box*, Do You Zoom Inc. USA

61. Tansley, T, tammytansley.com.au, 2014, *Taking the Angst Out of Work*, June 23 2014. Available from http://www.tammytansley.com.au/blog/taking-the-angst-out-of-work.html#.VKTz8MYz4hk [29 March 2015]

62. Fraser, A, 2012, *The Third Space: Using life's little transitions to find balance*, William Heinemann Book, Random House Australia, North Sydney, Australia

63. iHR Australia, 2015, *Sexist CEO offers employee "boob job": a case of misguided leadership,* April 2015. Available from: http://www.ihraustralia.com/hr-workplace-relations-news/sexist-ceo-offers-employee-boob-job-a-case-of-misguided-leadership) [24 April 2015]

Epitaph References

PART ONE

Matt Church (author of *Amplifiers*)

Church, M 2013, *Amplifiers*, Wiley, Queensland

Richelle E Goodrich (author)

Goodreads, 2015, *Quotes*. Available from: https://www.goodreads.com/quotes/1174473-you-are-here-to-make-a-difference-to-either-improve [23 April 2015]

Matt Church (author of *Amplifiers*)

Church, M 2013, *Amplifiers*, Wiley, Queensland

Gary Peterson (CEO, gap intelligence)

Peterson G, 2013, forbes.com, 23 April 2013. *The Four Principles of Followership*. Available from: http://www.forbes.com/sites/garypeterson/2013/04/23/the-four-principles-of-followership/ [23 April 2015]

PART TWO

C.G Jung (psychiatrist)

Goodreads, 2015, *Quotes*. Available from https://www.goodreads.com/quotes/3240-you-are-what-you-do-not-what-you-say-you-ll [23 April 2015]

Jon Allen (leadership and HR consultant)

Jon Allen via email with Tammy Tansley

George Bernard Shaw (author)

Brainy Quote, 2015, *Quotes*. Available from: http://www.brainyquote.com/quotes/quotes/g/georgebern385438.html [23 April 2015]

Ken Blanchard (author)

Blanchard, K, Carew D, Parisi-Carew E, 1990, *The One Minute Manager Builds High Performing Teams*, William Morrow and Company.

Rob Whitechurch (leadership and HR Consultant)

Rob Whitechurch via email with Tammy Tansley

Bill Gates (co founder of Microsoft)

Kasperkevic, J, inc.com. March 17 2013, *Good Feedback is the key to improvement*. Available from: http://www.inc.com/jana-kasperkevic/bill-gates-proper-feedback-is-key-to-improvement.html [23 April 2015]

John Russell (CEO of Harley Davidson)

The Aligned Career, 2015, *Quotes about Coaching*. Available from: http://thealignedcareer.com/quotes-about-coaching/ [23 April 2015]

Zig Ziglar (author)

Brainy Quote, 2015, *Quotes*. Available from: http://www.brainyquote.com/quotes/quotes/z/zigziglar387369.html [23 April 2015]

George S Patton (Soldier)

Brainy Quote, 2015, *Quotes*. Available from: http://www.brainyquote.com/quotes/quotes/g/georgespa106027.html [23 April 2015]

Barack Obama (President, USA)

New York Times, 2008, *Barack Obama's Feb. 5 Speech*. Available from: http://www.nytimes.com/2008/02/05/us/politics/05text-obama.html [23 April 2015]

PART THREE

Carol Dweck (author)

Dweck C, 2012, *Mindset: How You Can Fulfil Your Potential*, Constable and Robinson, UK Available from amazon.com [23 April 2015]

Seth Godin (author)

Godin, S 2014, *Linchpin*. Hachette Digital, Jouve, France. Available from amazon.com [23 April 2015]

George Eliot (author)

Brainy Quote, 2015, *Quotes*. Available from: http://www. brainyquote.com/quotes/quotes/g/georgeelio161679. html?src=t_never_too_late [23 April 2015]

PART FOUR

Donny Walford (Founder and Managing Director of DW Behind Closed Doors)

Donny Walford during interview with Tammy Tansley

Megan Quinn (Co-founder of net-a-porter)

Megan Quinn via twitter with Tammy Tansley

Donny Walford (Founder and Managing Director of DW Behind Closed Doors)

Donny Walford during interview with Tammy Tansley

Max Landsberg (author)

Landsberg, M 1996 *The Tao of Coaching* – Profile Books, London

www.ingramcontent.com/pod-product-compliance
Lightning Source LLC
Chambersburg PA
CBHW071548200326
41519CB00021BB/6658